THE BEST OF WRITERLOT

An Anthology
Volume One

I0537757

Edited by Girdharry

Contributors:

Alf Haywood

Alison Gardiner

Bill Webb

Bill "Boopadoo" Sauer

Cat Coffey

Colin F. Barnes

Gary Bonn

Girdharry

Island Writer

Issy Flamel

Janet Allison Brown

Louise Cole

Patrick LeClerc

Ren Warom

Steve Godden

Firedance Books

First published in the UK by Firedance Books in 2012.

ISBN: 978-1-909256-13-2

Firedance Books

firedancebooks.com

CONTENTS

ABOUT WRITERLOT

'WHY DON'T WE GET A GANG of great writers together and post a story from one of us each day? You know, on a website. I mean, wouldn't that be a great idea?'

The answer? WriterLot.net, which celebrated its first birthday in May 2012. On the site, a new piece goes up every day to fill your coffee time or to supply a bedtime story; everything from life on a Caribbean island through ghosts, romance, space-wars and humour.

The quality is always stunning.

After some arm-twisting and cajoling, we've put together this anthology of works snaffled from WriterLot's first year of creative endeavours. Sit back in a comfortable chair and snatch a few minutes of bliss away from the children screaming, the spouse spouting, the boss bossing, or the doctors frowning over your x-rays — and have fun.

When all is peaceful and the doctors have wiped the coffee stain off your x-rays, smile again and go to writerlot.net.

We promise you something new.

Gary Bonn, co-founder, WriterLot.net

PS: At WriterLot we honour the spelling and grammatical usage of whichever country our writer hails from. Just go with it...

CARDS

CAT COFFEY

'COUNTY CLERK'S OFFICE, THIS IS LAUREL, may I help you?'

Sarah took a deep breath and gripped the phone receiver. 'I'm getting divorced from a man who lives in your county, and he'll need to be served the paperwork, so I just need the address that I'll send the paperwork to, and how much it'll cost, and who to make the check out to.'

She took another breath and tipped the receiver away from her mouth to let it out.

'Aren't you going to long-arm it?'

Sarah paused. 'I don't know what you're talking about,' she half-laughed.

'Well, usually the sheriff doesn't do it,' Laurel said. 'In a divorce case, they long-arm serve the paperwork.'

She felt the tears welling, and viciously fought them back. With an almost-steady voice, she said, 'I'm just asking for the information my lawyer told me to get.'

'Well, here's the sheriff's number; you can give them a call, I guess.'

She scratched the number down quickly, and hung up before her voice could betray her.

'Why is this so damn difficult?' she asked between clenched teeth, willing the tears not to fall. She grabbed a tissue, a white flag signalling surrender in a battle she had lost so many times in the last two years. She wiped her eyes and marvelled again, for the hundredth time, at the sheer impossibility of ending the war.

Time and effort, she thought, and pulled a deck of cards from her desk. She slipped them from the box and spread them like a fan, then laid them down and took the top two. Using just her forefingers and thumbs to hold them, she set them endwise on her desk and leaned them against each other until the tops kissed, forming a tiny triangle.

For a long time — since leaving Duane, really — she had been growing increasingly fixated on the concept of time and effort as they related to construction and destruction. How it takes so much time to build a house of cards, but only an instant to destroy it; how it takes sweat and strain and muscles that want to tremble being held rock steady, to set each card in its perfectly-balanced place, but only an instant of misdirected breath to render all that labor useless. This counterbalance seemed to rule every aspect of observable life, from something as simple as the time taken to clean, fold, and press a shirt versus the instantaneous bump of a coffee cup that turned it into a thrift-store donation, all the way to something as complex as a human life, which could be twelve, twenty-eight, fifty-six years in the making, but could be wiped out in an instant by one guy changing the radio station when he should have been watching the intersection.

I guess I've found the exception that proves the rule, she thought bitterly, and made a second little triangle of cards next to the first.

It had taken her no time at all to get married. Called the court, walked in later that day with twenty-five dollars and a cheap bouquet, walked out married. Easy and quick as that. But divorce… Ye gods, even on amicable terms, without children or any marital assets, it was like pulling teeth to get the paperwork done.

So, she had begun to think, maybe the marriage was the house of cards falling down. Maybe the life she had before Duane, the years she had spent finding and making herself, was the careful stacking of slender cards. Maybe she was building her identity back up from the ground level, and that's why it was so hard.

Marriage is the destruction.

A soft rap at her office door, and she swept the cards into her lap and covered up the sheriff's number with another piece of paperwork. 'Yes?' She was already back to typing when the door cracked open and Leon's head appeared.

He smiled as he invited her to lunch with some other co-workers, and she smiled as she told him no thanks, got a bit backed up, I'll snack at my desk. His smile remained when he reminded her that Mr. Jameson better not catch her eating at her desk, and hers remained when she responded by dropping him a sly wink, knowing that Mr. Jameson would now almost certainly be dropping by to say hello.

'Ass-rag,' she said as soon as the door closed.

She looked again at the file she was updating, realized she had no idea what she was supposed to be typing, and bit back a scream. Instead of yanking the mouse out of its moorings and breaking it in half with her teeth, she clicked the little red "X" and told the computer not to save the file. Fuck it. She was taking lunch, and it would be a long one.

She locked her computer, pulled her sneakers from the bottom drawer of her desk, and traded them for the black pumps she was wearing. She considered her purse and rejected it in an instant. Instead, she pulled six dollars from her wallet and rode the elevator down eighty long stories with it tucked in the front of her bra. The halal vendor didn't even blink when she pulled it out to pay for a chicken gyro with extra red sauce. New York City, the place where no one cared where the money came from, as long it paid the bill. Glorious.

Sarah walked through the strangely quiet streets of the financial district, marvelling as always at the almost sepulchral feel of the high buildings of marble and stone. She ate as she walked, not bothering to wipe her mouth between bites. She wasn't out to impress anyone, not today.

She found herself wandering further than usual, and it was only when she was jostled for the third time that she realized she was moving through a crowd, and the crowd was converging on a familiar stretch of chain-link fencing. Plastic sheets draped the fence, all showing the same image: the new World Trade Center memorial site.

Sarah finished her gyro and chucked the wrapper in a garbage can, then worked her way through to the fence. The plastic drape was woven, and difficult to puncture, but a few enterprising souls had managed to punch holes in the photo landscape to see the real one beyond. She waited until one curious person moved aside, and she took his place, leaning forward to peer through the jagged opening.

It was a well-placed hole, with a sightline between two newly-planted trees and over the head-level of most of the throng beyond. It showed what she had seen on television a month before, the memorial that had the whole world sighing. But to Sarah, it was a horror. Who had ever conceived of this wretched idea? It was, quite literally, a hole in the ground.

Meant to be peaceful, she supposed, and maybe reflective, the memorial was a huge, square chasm with continuously flowing waterfalls cascading in a uniform sheet to the square pool far below. That water flowed in turn down into yet another square hole, this one seemingly bottomless, a black void that accepted the bright water and gave nothing back but darkness.

But water…water was life. In almost every cultural mythology Sarah could think of, it was equated with birth and renewal and the continuous flow of existence. So whose bright idea had it been to make a memorial that *swallowed life?* She shuddered.

A man looking through another hole nearby glanced over at her. 'You, too?'

She gave him a practiced, wary, New York glance. 'What?'

'It's creepy, right?'

'I guess. Yeah, it is.'

'You know you've got to have tickets to get in?' he asked, shaking his head. 'Tickets. Christ. It's not a fucking roller coaster, it's a graveyard.'

'And there's a line,' Sarah pointed out. 'A line for tickets to this.'

'They're free, but still.' He shrugged. 'That's pretty messed up.'

'From what I can tell, most things about this whole site can be described as "pretty messed up".'

'You ask me, they went the wrong way with this thing. They should've built something *up* at this place. Instead, they went *down.* That just doesn't seem right. It's like they did the opposite of building, you know?'

Sarah looked through the plastic sheet at the maw of rushing water and thought about construction and destruction again. Time and effort. Building things, and how long it took. Breaking them, and how easy it was. Negative space as a positive choice. Did it make sense at all?

'No, it really doesn't seem right,' she agreed. 'I think they took the easy way out.' *It's easier to break than to build. Easier to subtract. Time and effort.*

'You're not a vampire, are you?' the man asked, startling her.

Sarah's wariness returned. 'What?'

He brushed a finger on his chin and pointed to hers. 'You look like you've been going to town on an innocent virgin's neck there, a little bit.'

Sarah wiped her face and looked at the flaked remnants of spicy red sauce on her hands. 'No, no virgins for lunch. Actually, I've been eating a gyro.'

She pronounced it in the classic Greek fashion, so that it sounded like "hero," and it took only a second for the full, delicious irony of what she had said to hit her, and she burst into laughter. To her surprise, he did the same, and at the exact same moment.

He slapped at the fence, laughing. 'Which one? Ulysses?'

'No,' she chuckled, 'he was last week's meal. This one was Perseus.'

'I recommend Achilles. Tough, but edible if you start from the heel.'

Sarah laughed again. God, she loved New York City, where two random fans of Greek mythology could somehow stumble over each other like this.

They chatted for a few more minutes, during which Sarah learned that he was a philosophy professor at NYU who supplemented his income as a guide on one of the city's many walking tours. He'd been scouting this area for the most likely paths and times to bring a small group through.

When the two of them parted ways, he gave Sarah his business card.

"In case you'd like to learn more about our fair metropolis," he said. "Let me bore you some time with my extensive, highly specious analysis of the parallels between New York and Atlantis."

She wandered back to her office and changed back into her black pumps, looking at his business card on her desk and thinking about myths. His mention of Atlantis had stuck with her, and she was pondering the destruction of such an advanced and enlightened civilization in such a short and violent manner.

And by water. The symbol of life. The device of death.

It all hung together somehow, she was sure. There was something to understand in all of this. But what?

She held the card so that it stood on its edge and let it tip back and forth between her finger and thumb, falling to lean against one and then the other, back and forth. She could build a house of business cards, she mused, but it would take more than just one. Tap, tap. The card tipped back and forth. *Nothing stands on its own.*

She paused. *Or does it?*

On impulse, she bent the card in half and then released it, and now the card stood by itself, balanced on its single, thin edge in a V-shape by virtue of the physics of distributed momentum. Of course, it was no longer as pretty as it was, with a big crease down the middle and the puckered fibers of the cardstock poking out along its broken spine.

But it stood.

And only because it was broken could it stand alone.

Sarah blew the card onto its back and leaned over the creased face of it, reading the numbers there.

She picked up the phone.

Time and effort.

Reversed

Bill 'Boopadoo' Sauer

The Fool card from a tarot deck depicts a carefree wanderer, with a small dog who is either pestering him or, perhaps, warning him of an impending cliff edge. The upright Fool card represents a new beginning, a fresh start in any aspect of life — good luck. The reversed Fool card gives a clear warning that one must resist the temptation to act recklessly or immaturely in any new situation or possibly suffer bad luck.

I NEED A NEW DADDY-MAN. I had a good daddy-man, his name were Cedric. He'd play chase-ball with me, and scratch-the-belly, and share me bits of his meat and cheese every day. We went everywhere together, wet or bright, hot or cold, and he'd always find us nice places to sleep away the dark. Gallopy-horse houses full of hay for out of the cold, green grass hills under big trees for out in the warm. Me and my daddy-man, the world was our catch-ball. Until he met the bad lady.

I didn't like her; called me mangy. I don't know what mangy is, just that it ain't right and it ain't nice, because I'm a good boy. The daddy-man always told me so.

He'd say, 'You're a good boy, Little Man, come give the daddy kisses.'

The daddy-man didn't like when I yelled at the bad lady, but I needed to tell him she were bad. But she said, 'No mangy little bastards in my shop,' so the daddy-man made me stay outside, promised to be right back. He always promised to be right back, and then he would. I liked that, made me all wiggly-happy.

I found a climby-place round back, so I could get up to a look-in hole, the kind where you can see what's going on, but can't go through. The daddy-man and the bad lady sat at a table, looking at each other, and the bad lady put down cards with fancy pictures on them. I knows what cards is because the daddy-man taught me the game where I always pick the red queen-lady picture because it's the only one that always smells like cheese. Then all the two-legs laugh and pat my head and give the daddy-man shiny bits to put in his stick-sack. Then there'd be meat for dinner, and a chew-bone for me. I liked the card game days.

So the daddy-man and the bad lady are talking, and the bad lady is all mouth turned down, setting her cards with the pictures showing but not letting the daddy-man pick any. It didn't look like a fun game, and she just picked them all up again. The daddy-man opened his stick-sack and gave her some shiny bits, and then her mouth finally turned up. It wasn't a nice face she made; her teeth were happy, but her eyes were all mean and scheming. I started to shout, I had to warn the daddy-man.

'Daddy-man,' I cried, 'watch out for her! She smiles like a cat. Don't ever trust a cat!'

The daddy-man just yells, 'Shush, Little Man. I'll be right out.'

The bad lady touched his hand and he gets all mouth turned up and teethy, and then finally came out. I ran and hopped up and he caught me and I gave him kisses and he says, 'What's gotten into you, Little Man? I was only gone for a little while. And it's good news — life is going to get all rosy for us, real soon.'

I think "rosy" means the same as "good". I already thought life was rosy for us, but if the daddy-man is happier, I'm all wiggly-happy. We went to the place where all the two-legs eat and drink and get noisy, and had us some good games of red queen-lady. The daddy-man put lots of shiny bits, and a chew-bone for me, and some meat and bread and cheese in his stick-sack, and we found a good tree patch for dinnering.

After some good eats, I enjoyed some fine scratch-the-belly as the sky light began to go out, until I smelled her. The bad lady found us!

'Daddy-man, daddy-man,' I cried, 'we have to hide! Under the bramble bush with me!'

'What's wrong, Little Man?' he asked. 'What do you hear?'

I ran in circles, the small, fast danger-danger kind, so he might understand.

'Oh,' he said, 'it's just Madame LaFondue. You be a good boy, Little Man.'

'I am being a good boy!'

'There'll be none of what I came for with that mangy little bastard mucking about,' shrieked the bad lady. 'Tie it up to another tree over there.'

The daddy-man never, never tied me up before, but he listened to the bad lady. Why? Why would he do that to me? I were tail-down sad, I sat and whimpered and watched. The bad lady mashed her mouth against the daddy-man's, and then stepped back. That's when I heard the grass crunch — another two-leg, coming through the trees! I tried to warn the daddy-man again. The bad lady took the covering off her top half; the daddy-man ignored my yells and stared at her. A big-man two-leg came from behind and put a sack over the daddy-man's head, pulling it back to him. I cried and cried and tugged at the rope. The bad lady threw a stone at me while the big-man two-leg danced with the daddy-man. When the daddy-man grew too tired to dance anymore, they took the sack from his head and set him to sleep against the tree. They took all the shiny bits from his stick-sack but left the meat and cheese and cards and my chew-bone and catch-ball, and ran away.

I tried to wake the daddy-man with shouts, but he wouldn't. I spent all dark long chewing the rope, and when the sky light came back, I tried to wake him with kisses, like I always do. He just wouldn't. I ate the meat and cheese, but I left some for the daddy-man. I slept for a little while. When the sky light grew bright and hot, I tried to wake him again. He just wouldn't. Then I knew it — he weren't dark-sleeping, he were no-goodbye, no wake-up sleeping. Why didn't the daddy-man listen to me? I told him she were bad.

Now I need a new daddy-man, or maybe a mama-lady. How about you? Do you like to play cards?

PHILE ME UNDER TECHNOPHOBE

ALISON GARDINER

TECHNOLOGY ESCAPES ME. I'm quite sure I was put on this earth with the expected number of gigabytes in my brain and that, through the years, I've gathered enough info to make the whole system workable. However, I find that faced with clicky boxes, blank screens and techno things which should work and absolutely won't, the brain completely sags, cerebration shuts down, RAM fails. My neurones won't neur.

Work I can deal with. Give me a pile of problems, things that don't add up, difficult decisions and apparent dead ends and I'm in my element. At home the same. Problem solving R me. Yet, faced with technology that won't do what it's supposed to, I find myself cursing and making death threats to an inanimate object. Like it cares.

My one redeeming feature is that I show no bias at all in my dislike; technology in all its forms is beyond me. I discovered about a week ago how to close the small back windows in a car I've owned for 8 years. In fairness, we wouldn't normally open them in England, keeping them closed so ferrets, rabbits and hobbits can't get in. In France and at 36°C, it was different. Kids get very vocal if overheated. Small space, irritated offspring; best avoided. The little windows stayed open for six days 'til I figured the closing mechanism out. (Yup, only one button.) Kids cool though.

The television/DVD player is a complete mystery. In the days of an 'on' button and four channels: no problem. Four hundred and forty two options leave me calling for the kids to make it work.

Doubtless much of this is Freudian, as I have no real desire to know how to fix my own computer/printer/reprogram TVs. This is backed up by the fact that the photocopier regularly has a fugue and won't work. But I need it. I now have an intimate knowledge of its inner recesses and can fix most of its glitches. Sigmund would have been proud of the conveniently patchy nature of my mind fog.

Techno terminology doesn't help. I accept that every specialised area needs its own vocabulary but to me *mouse over* seems like the death of a rodent and *gigabyte* more like a snack at a concert. I've tried to tune in to the computer boffins fixing something but, once they've gone past the words 'Let's have a go at…', it appears that they are speaking Mandarin, perhaps insulting my grandmother or maybe offering me a recipe for duck and noodle cake.

The more I feel that I really should do something about it, the greater my complacency becomes, like accelerated apathy. Question is: do I really care?

I was cheered up by a text which I received yesterday from my husband on whom I rely for much of the technical input in the house. It read:

Noé on the stadium. Semés To havé Home. Intolérant spamish. À

Victim of Spanish keyboard/predictive text combi. I'm not alone.

Perhaps my brain needs defragging. However, I am concerned that if all the junk was removed, there would be very little serious stuff remaining to hold everything in some sort of order. Although it could be fun to switch with somebody else's brain to see what the inside of their head looks like and how their processing works. I'm convinced that there'd be huge market on eBay for a cerebral swap.

Brain for sale. One careful owner. In good shape for its age but needs a bit of reprogramming. Can stall and shut down completely. Bit grey; does it matter?

HEMLOCK'S HERESY #1 – PATRICIDE

COLIN F. BARNES

A near future utopia sounds nice, huh? Wouldn't everyone want to live and work in a Utopian society where the governing class is a group of highly respected and skilled philosophers who put the needs of the human wellbeing as top priority? Sure you would, and you'd be happy to be a registered Member Of Society in a perfect world where oil and industry have been replaced with sustainable and non-environmentally impacting organic machines. You might think all this wonderful, but under the surface there are those that suspect the Philosophers aren't all they're cracked up to be; there are those, like The Shades, who live off the grid and seek to live their own lives as individuals as opposed to cogs in a greater philosophical machine. Harrison Hemlock is one of those, but unlike his father, he doesn't have the talent for what The Shades deal in — but he'll have to learn fast as The Shades have plans for him.

PERSEPHONE, NAKED AND SWEATY, PURRED into Harrison's ear. 'I killed your father. He had some last words for you.'

Her hand gripped his erection. Stroked.

'"You're the last Hemlock. The burden is yours,' he said. 'You have to find that which I couldn't.'"

Fast strokes. Event horizon. One more beyond and he came. Deep shudders crashed through his spine like a direct injection of LiquidCrank. Spirals of colour exploded in his vision. He forgot to breathe. Kept coming in long powerful pulses. Her hand gripped him tighter, squeezing out the last of his essence.

Hot tongue licked his lobe. She whispered, 'He said the five Tomes are real, Marlowe has evidence.'

The Tomes are real?

His orgasm died. Cut short. Even the effects of the BloodStim couldn't prevent the premature sobering. Harrison's brain tried to comprehend. Failed. Too much to handle.

Limp, he eased away from Persephone. Left her sprawled on the sheepskin rug. Sweat gleamed on her brown skin. Illuminated by the single red lamp in the otherwise dark room. He tripped backwards, jeans bunched around his ankles. Head cracked against tiled floor. A lightning storm of pain thundered in his ears. *Goddamn!*

She let out a shrill laugh. Stood, moving like a snake. Muscles rippled beneath glossy skin. Her fierce, raven-coloured bob swayed as she stood astride him. Sharp, chrome-stilettoed boots rose up to her thighs. A Brazilian strip led his eye to her crotch. He stirred. But he remained flaccid.

'The Tomes are real? You fucking with me?'

Her eyes grew wide, pitch-black orbs reflecting the meagre light. She raised a boot, placed the sharp tip of the stiletto against his balls. 'You suggesting I'm lying?'

Shrivelled, he backtracked. 'Hell no.'

'Hell no *what,* maggot?'

Really, still this act? He wondered if she was ever out of character, if this was a character. He'd only known her for a few weeks. She came highly recommended by one of his more nefarious clients. 'Assassin and Dom. Equally efficient at both,' his contact said.

The stiletto pushed further into the soft flesh of his testicles.

'OK. Hell no, Mistress.'

'That's better. Now, you gonna help a girl with papa's body?'

'I paid extra for disposal.'

'He struggled. Made a mess of the lab. You said he would be ready to go.' Persephone raised a thin, sculpted eyebrow. Placed a hand on her hip. Struck a pose full of harsh angles.

Light from the red lamp reflected off her metal boot-heels. Struck the gloom like neon warning signs. More weapons than footwear. He remembered the story of how she punctured a guy's eyeball with a single swift kick. He no longer doubted its validity.

'Fine. I'll help. Just let me take that to the freezer first,' Harrison pointed to a sample cup on the rug. 'Those little guys need to be preserved.'

Persephone smiled. Straight white teeth gleamed. Unnatural. Incisors sharpened. Perfect for puncturing a vein. *Is that how she killed dad? A deadly kiss. Those same lips that...* he shook his head. Too fucked up to contemplate.

Persephone picked up the cup of ejaculate. Handed it to him. 'Didn't miss a drop of your precious honey, little bee.'

It all counted. The success percentile shrunk week by week, he needed every single sperm for testing. 'I'm outsourcing the production of my replacement organs. Something's changed.'

'Philosophers infiltrated your little alchemy lab?'

'No. I don't know what it is. My DNA is breaking down in the cloned organs.'

'Why not just replace with synthetic? Last longer than you'll live.'

'It's junk. Dead inert junk.' Synthetic meat. Damned Philosophers' answer to everything since they took over the government. Medicine, transport, infrastructure. They'd gone too far. Forgotten what it was to be human. But not Harrison. Even his replacement hand was old-fashioned carbon-fibre, none of this synthetic bullshit.

Persephone stepped away. Wrapped a black robe around her lithe body. 'You mind if I switch the heating on?'

'No, thermostat's down the hall.' He watched her ass sway as she drifted down the white marbled corridor and out of the open-plan living area. A low rumble, like horses running, vibrated up from the basement. The thought of those synthetic muscle-units turning the heating dynamo made him think of the butcher's shop as a kid. Red slabs of fleshy meat. Thick crimson hunks flecked with blue and white sinewy veins.

Meat's replaced everything.

He preferred honest mechanical materials from the old days: steel, carbon, iron, oil. Anything but muscle-tissue and PowerGrain stomach systems. *No going back now that oil's dried up.*

Sharp clacks echoed on white tiles as Persephone sauntered back into the room. She walked like a supermodel: hips swaying, shoulders high, toes pointing forward. Indomitable. Invincible. *And she knows it.*

'You look a bit like him. You know that?'

'How so?' Harrison didn't believe he looked much like his father at all. Grew up thinking he was adopted.

'You have his eyes, almost grey, like they've been bleached. You're tougher than him though. You don't have his delicate poise.'

'I had to be tough. No one around to look after me. Dad spent most of his time making you bastards weapons, FleshNet traffic syphons, and God knows what else.'

'Poor little Harrison. By the way, you're nearly out of PowerGrain.'

'I know. Dad usually orders it. I guess it's up to me now.' He knew there should be guilt there. But there wasn't, just a feeling of sadness and inevitability. The great 'individualist' Charles Hemlock, scourge of the Philosophers, had been dying. Irreversible cancer. Harrison had just made it less public, put him out of his misery. And the money would be useful.

'They were going to use him, you know that? Everyone thinks they are so perfect, so reasonable. Those damned Philosophers planned to use dad as an example of the dangers of individualism. But do you think any of those assholes out there, those mindless drones would see that it was bullshit? Or that it's they themselves that perpetuate this sham of a society that withheld his treatment,revoked his rights. It's them that killed him.'

Persephone lit a hand-rolled cigarette. Sat on the glass dining chair and leaned back against the table. The same table Harrison and his father used to sit at and talk about the Tomes, the possibilities, the potential of an individual.

The Tomes: five books written by a single, unnamed man. The ultimate individualist.

Growing up, Harrison always thought it was bollocks. Just stuff his dad would talk about to stop him joining the Members Of Society. 'Underneath all this utopia is a rotten core. They've forgotten what it is to be human. We are more than just Members of Society,' he used to say, always at the end of their conversations.

The Tomes themselves were rumoured to have unparalleled insight and guidance into the human condition. Details and specifics for an individual to rise through the hierarchy of needs and become transcendent: ultimately human.

Harrison enjoyed the idea of them, but considered them myth. Still, they intrigued him; so he would sit and listen to his father explain their importance. It was part of the reason why his father worked with the Shades Guild. Like the Knights of the Round Table, it was their quest to find them. Or at least it used to be a decade ago. These days they were more interested in making wet-tech devices for the rich or the insane. Surveillance, weaponry, pleasure. Anything anyone with enough cash could think of.

That was Charles Hemlock's great talent. The melding of flesh and technology. Anything you could imagine he could build it. He was a great wet-tech. A true MeatPunk. The talent wasn't hereditary though. Harrison wanted no part of it. Preferred good, honest bootlegging and thievery.

'Where are we moving his body to?' Harrison pulled up his jeans and buttoned a black shirt. Pure cotton. One of a kind. There was no cotton anymore. Only synthetic fibres. Needed the crop space for food and PowerGrain.

'The pipes. Marlowe will meet us at the corner of Aphex and Burke and take us down. He'll take your father's brain and heart — '

'Naturally.'

'Marlowe's working on a new construction — a weapon of sorts. Designed by your father. The rest will go into the recycler.'

A judder crept down his spine at the thought of that — device. So much organic matter had gone through the recycler: chewed with NuBone teeth, digested, and shitted out into constituent organic material for repurposing. Like his hand.

Caught for stealing as a teenager, Marlowe had forced it into the recycler as punishment. Harrison could never tell dad though. Marlowe was like his brother. Charles spent more time with Marlowe and the Shades than with his own family.

Old Charlie would be a part of everything the Shades made for at least a week. Ironic really. Still, it's an honour of sorts. Better than being dumped in a shallow grave filled with calcium oxide. Like his mum.

'Will you miss him?' Persephone asked.

An interesting question. He genuinely didn't know. It was a mercy killing, but not through any deep-rooted love or affection. It was to stop his family name being ground into the dirt by the Philosophers. Especially now that he was the last Hemlock. Sure, there was some pity there. Who couldn't feel pity for a man being eaten away from the insides while refusing synthetic replacements? Marlowe even offered to do it. Had them ready to go. But like Harrison, Charles had no interest in fake, petri-dish organs. Preferred cloned, even if they were still diseased. 'All part of being human,' he used to say.

'You listening to me? Will you miss the old guy?'

'Do you care?'

'No. I'm just making polite conversation. I'm kind like that.'

'That cost extra?'

'Manners never cost extra, Harrison. You'd do well to remember that in your new job.'

He snorted. 'Job? What job?'

Those sharp, dangerous teeth gleamed again. Exposed by smiling lips. 'Aw, you didn't know. How precious.'

'What are you talking about?'

'You thought Dad's estate would come to you. You were wrong.'

'I saw the will.'

Persephone smiled. Stood. Click-clacked her way across the tiled floor to stand just inches from his face. 'You're mine now, little Bee. Daddy left his estate to the Shades. You have a salary waiting. And you owe us. Somebody needs to take up the slack now Daddy's not around.'

'Fuck the Shades. Fuck you. I ain't working for you lot.'

Turning on her heel, Persephone headed down the corridor. Spoke over her shoulder, 'Your first job was to dispose of the body. I guess the police can help you with that. Shame DNA is so prevalent in murder enquiries these days. And it would be terribly inconvenient if they were to find your bootlegging stash. What's that, a twenty stretch inside?' She trailed off with a hint of a laugh.

Fuck! Double Fuck.

* * * *

Down a winding, steel staircase, the lab was two floors below the lounge. Their decor style wasn't dissimilar. Both shared white marble-tiled floors and clean minimalist lines. The walls in both were spartan. The lounge featured a few select pieces of art. The lab had its own kind of art: images of organs in cross section: human, animal, and other unique constructions. His father's work. Those images had burned their way into Harrison's mind for years. He knew every line, every label.

Entering the lab, Harrison was transported back twenty years; his father holding him close as they entered a local butcher's. Image: a fat man with a red-streaked smock standing behind a counter holding a meat cleaver in one hand and a long piece of lamb's neck in the other. The butcher's shop always reeked of blood, and empty drinks cans: mild, metallic, and a little sweet.

Image: swift arc of the cleaver. A dull chop as metal hits wood. A small spray of blood, which would later bloom into a blurry starburst on the thin paper wrapping containing the meat. It was never for dinner though. Charles Hemlock would send Harrison upstairs where Mother was waiting. For years, Harrison thought his dad was eating alone in his lab while he and Mother ate in silence at the dining table.

Now fifteen: Harrison opens the door to the lab, curiosity of his father's activities growing too strong to ignore.

Red everywhere. On the walls, the tiles, the stainless steel work surface. His dad: a butcher. A blood covered smock wrapped around his tall, thin body. Scalpel in one gloved hand, soldering needle in the other.

Current day: the room is much the same. Blood on the walls, the tiles, the work surface. His dad, wearing the same smock: blotched with gore formed into myriad nebulae.

Harrison bent over his father's corpse. His skin, grey and sallow, hung on a thin, cancer-ravaged body. His muscle mass had atrophied. Eaten away. And yet, he worked until his last day. Scalpel in one hand, an organic device half finished on the workbench. It looked like a pig's heart. Copper wires inserted into veins, joined to a PowerGrain battery converter. Nanotube lattice covered it like an exoskeleton. No idea what the hell it was or did. *Like most of things he made.*

'Couldn't you have been cleaner?' An ugly wound punctured his father's neck. Ragged skin torn around two rough holes. 'You fucking bit him. No wonder this place is a mess.'

Persephone leaned back against the workbench inspecting her ruby varnished nails. Smiled.

'I paid you to fucking respect him. Do it quick and painless, I said.' Harrison's good hand trembled as he crushed it into a fist. Knuckles blazed white. Threatened to burst out of reddening skin.

'So you care after all?'

He was about to leap over the body and strike her when she lifted a leg. Pointed the sharpened stiletto at his throat. 'Calm down, honey bee.'

He skidded on the slick floor, regained his balance and took a step back. 'Calm down? This was supposed to be about preserving his dignity.'

'He struggled. I needed to act quickly.' Persephone turned her back. Displayed an ugly gash between her shoulder blades.

Where was the blood? The wound was open. Skin curled at the edges.

Oh shit. Persephone smiled again, seemingly her default reaction to anything and everything, which now made sense.

'You're a fucking automaton. Aren't you? One of Marlowe's creations.'

'Not quite. You'll have a chance to ask him though. Now grab daddy's legs, we need to get going.'

* * * *

They pulled up to a designated parking space on the corner of Aphex and Burke. The dynamo of Persephone's car — designed and built by Marlowe; the lack of any interior comfort was a signature of his — whined down, creating an animal-like cry. Harrison could never get comfortable with the meat engines. Genetically modified muscle working in sync with electronically controlled propulsion systems just didn't seem right.

It was anachronistic to have this aversion, but he couldn't help thinking it was going too far, this reliance on 'wet-tech'. Perhaps it was the noise, or lack of it. He was just about old enough to remember internal combustion engines and their throaty roar. These meat engines were so different. Thick, red, ropey muscle pulled and pushed in silence.

At night, one could creep up on you and you would never know it was there.

'Friendly round here, aren't they?' Persephone said, referring to Harrison's neighbour offering to help them load their 'heavy item'.

'What do you expect from a Member Of Society? Nosey bunch. Ignore them, don't engage, they'll only try and convert you to the Philosopher's way.'

'Oh, honey, you're forgetting who you're talking to. I deal with the MOS on a daily basis.'

Harrison knew exactly what she meant by 'deal with,' and it wasn't holding polite conversation.

The corner of Aphex and Burke was like any of the street corners: quiet dirt roads forming a strict grid pattern. Between the roads, PowerGrain fields stretched as far as the eye could see. No more cities any more. All rural.

In the distance, a rolling thin cloud of dirt swirled into the sky. It was getting late, nearly dusk. The sun dipped beyond the horizon. Pink and orange tones lit the underside of clouds like melted tropical fish.

The sound of his breathing seemed excessive in the stillness. Persephone had one elbow resting on the door. She smoked with the other hand. Smiling.

Marlowe will be here soon.

He flexed the fingers of his replacement hand unconsciously. He still had those phantom feelings as if his real fingers were still there.

His throat was dry, and a dread crept through his bowels. He clenched his good hand. Fidgeted in the car seat. Awaited Marlowe's arrival.

The last thing Marlowe had said to him — after 'recycling' his hand — was a vow to remove his eyeballs and make them into a jewellery piece for the Philosophers.

He reminded himself to breathe. To relax. To be rational. It didn't work. He kept on grinding his teeth. Cracking his knuckles. Tapping a foot. Anything to extinguish the nervous energy.

And the fear.

What would Marlowe's reaction be now that Harrison had his best friend and best wet-tech killed? *Can't be anything good.*

A black, sleek, curved vehicle approached. Stopped. Dust covered the bodywork. To anyone else it would look like any other car. But from behind the windscreen, two green orbs glowed from inside the dark cabin.

'Marlowe's here.' Persephone whispered. Blew a smoke ring as she exhaled.

Goddamned Marlowe.

More of ***Hemlock's Heresy*** is available at **www.writerlot.net**

Make a Wish

Gary Bonn

HER LONG CURLS STRAIGHTEN as she leaps and they fly up into a sunlit halo at the height of her jump. Arm outstretched, she snatches at the fluttering leaf and misses. She lands, the woodland floor crackling under her sandals.

I think she's about eight years old. The boy, maybe six; he's running, face turned to the air above, arms stretched up in a V shape. The second little girl is about two or three; she stands and watches, like she doesn't know what to do.

Squeaks, yelps and giggles pursue the golden leaves as they spin and tumble. The older girl shouts in triumph and holds a leaf, snatched from the air, to her bowed forehead, closes her eyes and mouths silent words. She looks up again into the autumn cascade. The boy misses a catch, scoops the leaf from the ground and throws it towards the little girl. She giggles and picks up a tight fistful. Holding it towards the boy, her body and arm jerk. The leaves fall from her hand and scatter. She doesn't know how to throw yet.

Sunlight. Sunlight so bright. It adds life, makes things more real. Trees can be so huge, so vast. Why is everything so super-real, so vivid?

Of course. My chest tightens, my left arm burns; my heart lacks oxygen.

My fingers, thin and covered with loose blue-blotched skin, rise from the arm of the wooden park bench and reach for the tablets in my top pocket. I'll take two — if I can get them under my tongue in time. Tremor and the pain slow me down, I'm clumsy and rushed: fumbling. I want to watch the children.

Even if I called an ambulance it would never arrive in time. The pain diminishes. It's more numbness now, but it probably isn't the tablets working. One is stuck on my denture and I don't know where the other went. The world looks brighter, more beautiful than ever. Darkness creeps in from the edge of my vision.

The taller girl captures a spinning leaf. She pirouettes and whoops; her hair flies out, wraps around her face for a moment, and falls shimmering. She runs to the little girl who waits with outstretched hands. The dimpled knuckles of the very young. The leaf drops; the boy rescues it before it hits the ground and pushes it into the chubby hands.

The little one waves it. The others are telling her to close her eyes. 'Make a wish!'

A PROMISE FULFILLED

GIRDHARRY

B EFORE STEPPING THROUGH THE GATEWAY, I look back, regarding the early morning mist of my forever dream. For a moment a vision hangs in the air; a place I've never visited, always longed to know. My imaginary land of Guyana. By night, a fragment of me wanders there, lost.

A country with a South American and a Caribbean pulse. Home of my parents. I remember a yellow and blue handkerchief woven with a map. As a child, I loved to trace the wavy, coastal line with my finger, gazing at the pink coconut-ice place names. A dear treasure, but lost. Thrown out by a thoughtless adult? Maybe. I locked my tears away together with a promise.

The long wait is almost over. Tomorrow, I shall let my promise fly free across the continents. I shall let the rhythm of that land at last resonate with my blood. Drenching myself in the rainforest, I shall call back the lost fragment. Whether she will come or not, I cannot tell you. What I can say is, however bitter or sweet the taste of the real Guyana, the child in me will rejoice.

THE ISLAND – EPISODES FROM PARADISE

ISLAND WRITER

Island Writer produces non-fiction pieces about life on the tropical island of Antigua, West Indies.

When it rains

STRANGE THINGS HAPPEN WHEN IT RAINS. There are clouds overhead most days. I remember when we first arrived, how surprised I was at the number of clouds. I guess I'd imagined predominantly clear, blue skies. The clouds form quickly. You can watch it happen with the naked eye and high-level winds carry them across the island. There's a great deal of low-level wind too… it makes for great sailing. No wonder they call these islands the Windies — short, of course, for the West Indies. Rarely are the days windless — thank goodness. The heat and humidity would be tough to deal with otherwise. Temperatures are pretty steady throughout the year, hovering around 77° f (25° c) to 82° f (28° c) with 75-85% humidity. It's the humidity that's hardest. The sweat pours off your body even when you're standing still. If you live on the east coast of the island, you get the cooling winds from the Atlantic. Many people prefer it to the west, but personally, I'd rather see the incredible sunsets, which we enjoy in Jolly Harbour. Sunrise is a special time too, with colours drifting over the horizon, but it's more subtle.

When it does rain here, it's a downpour, heavy and sudden and it stops as quickly as it starts. It never lasts long and if you're caught outside, sheltering under a tree will only delay you for a few minutes. Umbrellas are useful, but they need to be strong enough to handle the power of the deluge. I bought a cheap one when I was back in the UK last year and it broke the first time I used it in a tropical downpour — they just aren't built for the force of the rain and wind! There's no such thing as drizzle here.

The locals down-tools when it rains. They never work in the rain. I walk in the rain — it's cooling. I've seen some rolling of the eyes as I stride past, head down, baseball cap on, pushing through the rain to my destination. One day a local called out, 'You crazy lady, why you walk in de rain?' When I replied, 'It's only water.' I got back a bemused stare.

On the rare occasions when the sky is grey and overcast and the rain is on and off all day, the whole island reacts. People get nervous. They stay at home. They don't venture out if it's raining too hard. It has everything to do with poor or non-existent drainage.

When the ground is already waterlogged, the water has nowhere to go. Similarly, if there hasn't been rain for a while, the ground can't absorb it fast enough. When roads aren't paved, stones and rocks are carried along gullies and deposited where they land. The access road to our last apartment was so poorly constructed, the tarmac was eaten by the fast-flowing rainwater cascading downhill. Within a day or two, it no longer looked like a paved road but a dried-out riverbed complete with mud, stones and boulders.

One of the problems is the lack of heavy machinery needed to build a road. The Chinese were brought in to build roads for the Cricket World Cup, bringing their knowledge and machinery with them. They did a great job, but laying good roads is expensive. Patching is what Antiguans do best, and patching is what they'll continue to do, but it never lasts.

Proper road building should be a priority. The main road from the airport to St John's and from St John's down the west coast is the main artery for traffic and it's strewn with potholes. If the locals have to drive in the rain, they crawl along as if afraid the puddle they're driving through may be a pothole large enough to swallow them whole. There's a joke here — if you're driving in a straight line, you must be drunk. If you were sober, you'd swerve to avoid the potholes.

When the sky is grey and rain is pounding, the temperatures drop and vigorous activities become much more comfortable. Many babies are conceived on these days — they're known as 'Days for Lovers'. Schools close early and children are sent home because the buses may not make it along the flooded roads. (It's like 'snow days' when we lived in Scotland.)

Many won't even bother to turn up to work if rain is forecast. Most local-style homes are built of wood and are up on breeze blocks so water runs under the house instead of flooding through it. It's a good idea. It also keeps out some of the creatures that scuttle inside when it rains.

All creatures great and small

Now that we're on the ground floor of a house, we witness some of these creatures first hand. Just last week a grey land crab climbed up the mosquito netting on the screen door outside our bedroom after a heavy downpour and we found it clinging to the top of the door frame in an extraordinary feat of agility. When we tried to move it, it waved its pincers at us angrily. We eventually got it down by whacking it with a broom but it pulled the mozzie netting with it, perhaps in a final act of defiance.

Some of the land creatures here are huge. Much bigger than we're used to in the UK. The frogs, for example, are gnarled and knobbled. Even the island dogs are afraid of them. One night I went down to feed the guard dogs at our last home and wondered why they hung back. Normally they'd devour food the moment their bowls hit the ground. I scanned the area with a torch, and what I saw made me gasp. A prehistoric-looking creature covered in warts, crouched ten feet away — a frog the size of my laptop (and I'm not talking about a netbook here either). It was Jabba the Hutt, in the flesh. It had to weigh 5lbs. It sent a shiver through me. It wouldn't move, it's huge eyes staring blankly while the dogs cowered and I stood in shock. I had to put their food bowls out of the frog's line of sight before they'd eat. When I went back to check on the dogs, Jabba had lumbered away, never to be seen again. I was glad we lived on the top floor on that occasion!

I did some research. It wasn't a frog, but a Giant Neotropical Toad, introduced throughout the Caribbean as a method of agricultural pest control, especially for sugar cane, one of Antigua's main agricultural crops back in the days of slavery. Its skin is highly toxic to any animal that eats it.

Another strange creature appeared one evening as we came home from a rare dinner out. Hanging in the corner of the sitting room was an enormous black moth, its wings and body seemed almost velvety.

I swear I felt like a Lilliputian from *Gulliver's Travels*. Its wingspan was about a foot across and it clung to the wall and refused to budge. I couldn't watch... I've no idea how he did it, but my husband got it out of the house.

The scariest creature of all to come out after a heavy downpour is the tarantula. No kidding. We'd been warned about them before we left the UK but I'd never seen one up close, until recently. When it rains, the steady beating of rain on the ground brings them out. I guess they figure there's a party going on... the beat of the drums shakes their holes!

A field we used to cross as a shortcut had recently been cleared of bush and was bare soil until grass and foliage regrew. There were holes in the ground everywhere. These were tarantula holes and we christened the field, The Tarantula Field. They must have had a veritable city of tunnels. It reminded me of Roald Dahl's *The Fantastic Mr Fox*. It was disturbing to think of tarantulas inches below our feet as we walked... so the day I saw a dead tarantula after the rains came, was the day I stopped using the short cut!

Then I came face to face with a live one... just writing about it sends shivers down my spine. It was on a pane of broken glass at the gym. Luckily, we were on different sides of the glass. It was huge. I couldn't get too close but I could clearly see its chunky, hairy legs that no doubt ended in Dr. Martens, four pairs, surrounding a thick body. Uuugghh.

Even the bees are different here — surprisingly, they're smaller than the humble British bumblebee. One day, I noticed a lot of them hovering just outside the bedroom window. It was most disconcerting, knowing they were inches from my bed, separated only by a window-mounted mosquito screen. I watched in fascination as more and more bees arrived and left, all day long. There was no sound, no heavy buzzing, but they were busy with something. There was purpose to their activities.

Then I realised why they were there. They'd built a hive inside an old air-conditioning duct. It's laughable really, how even the bees will use something else rather than go to the trouble of building their own hive.

As the weeks went by, I grew used to their presence and I watched them as I worked at my desk by the window. Antiguan bees are slow-moving, just like the people. They don't seem to live long either — I'd often find dead ones littering the balcony and I stood on one by mistake. Except it wasn't dead... resting perhaps. It stung me. Curious to see what kind of reaction my body would have, I waited. The pain of the sting dissipated after a few minutes. It itched, but not much. Most surprising of all was the lack of swelling. I remember standing on a bee at the swimming pool as a child and how my foot swelled up so much I couldn't wear a shoe. In Antigua, they're just too lazy to sting much or to buzz!

Haggis Comes Home

Janet Allison Brown

'HE'S JUST STANDING THERE,' she said. 'In the middle of his room. Again.' She flumped down onto the sofa. 'I tried to make him sit down at least, but he wouldn't. Would it really hurt him to give a little? Would it?'

'Give him time,' said Clyde, rubbing her shoulders.

'We've given him time. He's been here ten bloody weeks.'

'At least he's talking to us now.'

Esther rolled her eyes ceiling-wards. 'No, he's talking at us. There's a difference.'

'At least he's talking,' said Clyde.

'Well he's still not listening. Whenever I talk to him he just stares at me.'

Clyde's thumb found a knot just inside her right shoulder blade. 'Are you regretting it?' he asked gently.

'No,' she said, pulling away and turning to face him. 'Hell, no, Clyde. Of course not! It's just...I didn't think it would be...like this.'

'It's early days.'

'I know,' she said gloomily, taking his hand as he came to sit beside her. 'But each day has twenty-four hours in it, and each hour has sixty minutes and each minute has sixty seconds. It adds up.'

* * * *

The room was pretty big and there was stuff, just loads of it, everywhere. Joshua hadn't made sense of it yet. Every time Esther came in and moved stuff around, he had to start his mental inventory again. At least she was leaving him alone more often these days, although she still had a tendency to pop her head around the door whenever she felt like it. He'd have to sort that out. A timetable — that might work. He'd give her a timetable so he'd know when she was coming.

He had the bed sorted. He'd folded the blanket seven different ways to see what worked best. She kept shaking it out in the morning, of course, but he could already put that right in under two minutes.

The wicker basket still troubled him. It was full — full full full — of stuff. He'd tried organising it. At the end of the first week he'd emptied it out onto the floor and started putting things into piles.

'What are you doing?' Esther had asked. Her voice was too high — he registered that — but her face wasn't wearing one of the expressions he recognised. Her features were not open wide in happiness, admittedly, but neither were they squished into the centre of her face in anger. He decided it was safe to be honest.

'I don't want these,' he'd said, pointing to one of the piles. 'The rest is okay, but it should be on the shelf. You can take the basket.'

Her face stiffened. She turned and left the room.

A few minutes later she returned and put everything back into the wicker basket. 'This is where toys belong,' she'd said, taking charge. 'And you must keep everything. You don't know what you'll feel like playing with tomorrow.'

Joshua stared at the wicker basket. It was bewildering. How could he sleep with this chaos in the room? He'd have to think of some way to impose order, something that wouldn't make Esther's eyes go squinty and red; he'd recognised *that* look.

He crossed the room and moved the green corduroy chair an inch to the left, so that the mid-afternoon sun landed exactly in the centre of the seat. In about three minutes it would need adjusting again. He would stand there and wait.

* * * *

'We spent hours and hours choosing all those toys and setting up his room,' Esther complained, wiping her eyes. 'I know. I'm the grown-up. It's not about me. What is that?'

Clyde put the cardboard box down on one end of the kitchen table. Esther had begun to set the table and wanted to move it, but he stopped her: 'Let him do it.'

Joshua came downstairs. They sat down and Esther served dinner.

Joshua said nothing, but he didn't eat, either. Finally he pointed at the box. 'Shall I move that off the table?'

Clyde put a restraining hand on Esther's knee. 'Sure,' he said.

Joshua respectfully picked up the box — he was still painfully respectful — and put it on the floor. Then he sat down and began to eat. But apparently all was not well. After a few mouthfuls he put down his knife and fork, stood up, and moved the box onto a chair.

Before the meal was over, he had shifted the box six times. His movements were becoming agitated.

'Let's look inside,' suggested Clyde, lifting the box onto the table. He held out a hand for Joshua, but Joshua wouldn't come. Clyde dropped his hand and began to open the box. 'Look, Esther, come and take a look.'

Esther peered inside and let out a soft cooing sound. 'Oh my God. Babies!'

Joshua took a step nearer; they ignored him.

'So sweet!' sang Esther. 'Can I hold one?'

'You're going to have to. They need feeding.'

Joshua watched intently as Clyde lifted out a little hoglet, pink and scrawny with a pointy nose and fuzz for prickles. He watched Clyde mix up some powder with warm water, test the temperature, and show Esther how to firmly hold the baby in one hand and syringe the liquid into its mouth with the other. Joshua reached into the box.

'Careful!' said Esther sharply.

Joshua dropped the creature abruptly and took a step backwards.

'It's okay,' she relented. 'You just have to be very gentle.'

Joshua did not try again. He watched for one polite minute more, then went up to his room.

'Sorry,' said Esther softly.

'Early days,' said Clyde, planting a kiss on her head.

* * * *

There were four hoglets and they needed feeding every few hours, around the clock. Joshua showed no interest in the first two feeds, stood by watching the third. When Esther rose at midnight for the fourth, quietly cursing this new project of Clyde's, she found Joshua sitting in the kitchen, a hoglet in one hand and a syringe in the other.

The milk was the perfect temperature. She stroked the boy's head and then quietly retreated.

'He remembered everything,' she whispered as she snuggled back down into bed beside Clyde. 'He's better at it than I am.'

'He's been watching pretty closely,' said Clyde.

She gave him a gentle kick. 'You think you're so smart.'

'Well,' he said into her hair, 'I am pretty smart.'

Their satisfaction took a knock next morning when they finally understood, after much shouting and many tears, that last night's events meant that Joshua had now taken sole charge of the hoglets and no one else was allowed to touch them.

'They're not yours!' Esther had shouted.

'But I kept them alive last night!' he shouted back.

'And you did a great job, but I was there too, remember? They wouldn't have died!'

'They're alive because I fed them,' he insisted. 'I do it better than you do. I hold them right. You hold them like this.' He mimed her actions; she recognised her own awkwardness and was enraged. Before she knew it, she was a wild thing, a harpy, a banshee.

Later, when she thought back on it, wincing with shame, she took some comfort in the fact that her fury hadn't affected him at all. He was a stone. A rock. She would crash and splinter against him if she wasn't careful.

* * * *

In the weeks that followed Esther lost control of many more things, starting with the water jug. It began with a little dance at breakfast over who should be the one to pour water for Clyde, erupted into a brief but violent struggle of wills, and ended when Esther decided that this was one battle she was prepared to lose. Which was a mistake, as she was reminded at every subsequent meal.

'Now he's lord of the water jug,' she said bitterly to Clyde. 'To lose a battle once is to lose it for all time. The trouble is, everything is a crapping battle, and every crapping battle gets written up in tablets of stone like the ten crapping commandments. Except there aren't just ten of them, Clyde, there are hundreds. Thousands.'

* * * *

The hoglets grew quickly under Joshua's care. He spent hours on the internet researching the care of orphaned hedgehogs, swapping notes and advice with other aficionados. In a short while he'd become an expert, dispensing cyber-advice like bubble-gum.

And then, quite suddenly, three of the babies died, one after the other in quick succession. Joshua was furious. 'I fed them right!' he shouted. 'I did everything right. Why did they die?'

'It was always a risk,' said Clyde. 'Babies aren't made to survive without their mother.'

'But I was looking after them! I would always have looked after them!'

Clyde shook his head, quaking inside — not at the deaths, which he'd half-expected, but at the impact on Joshua, which he hadn't.

* * * *

Joshua would not bury the little pink bodies. He wouldn't feed the remaining baby, who clung tenaciously to life. Esther took up the task. In a brief, weak moment, she found herself thinking, 'Ha, see? You don't rule the universe, Mister Joshua Poshua. And when the chips are down, who's here to pick up the pieces, huh?' With that out of her system, she reminded herself — again — that she was the adult and Joshua was the child, no matter how much he might try to reverse their roles. She tried to be very gentle, very kind to him, but he was impervious; he was a rock.

Haggis grew bristles and then spikes; Joshua wouldn't use his name, look at him, talk to him. They couldn't release Haggis because winter was coming on and he hadn't yet gained enough body fat to withstand the cold. Instead, Clyde built a roomy hedgehog house to shelter him for the winter months. But Haggis did not hibernate; he liked to be held, liked to run over the frost-spiked grass, liked to be fed. The sun grew milky and the days shortened and Haggis grew fat and lazy.

* * * *

Early next spring, Clyde came home from work to find Esther sobbing in bed.

'What happened this time?' he asked. He was tired. Tired from work, tired of holding things together day after day. One of them had to stay strong at all times, but really, he would have liked to drum his own heels on the floor now and then.

She lifted a smeared face to him. 'I had coffee with Irene today,' she said.

'That's nice.'

'She asked me if I loved him yet.'

Clyde heaved a sigh. 'We don't have time to handle other people's expectations,' he began. 'We made a deal, remember? We don't listen to what other people think.'

'No,' she said, putting a gentle finger on his mouth. 'Let me finish. I know love isn't enough. I know that.'

'Commitment is what counts,' he said.

'I know. And I started to say that to her, and then I realised: I love him. I do. I know we've changed nothing. He'll never call us mum and dad, and even if he did, it wouldn't mean anything. He'll probably never hand us control of his world, and it might never get easier. But I love him anyway.' She started to laugh and it was a light sound, not bitter or ironic, not a grasping for the silver lining. This was the sound of sleigh-bells on a frosty night, or a bird's wings flapping on a quiet morning — a real sound, nothing more or less than itself, but capable of igniting lightning in the soul.

A piercing wail came from the garden. They ran outside and found Joshua beside the hedgehog house. The lid was open and the house was empty.

'He's gone!' screamed Joshua. 'You didn't close the door properly! You didn't keep him safe!'

'Joshua,' began Clyde, reaching out a hand. 'It's spring. It was nearly time to release him anyway.'

'But we didn't release him! He escaped! It's not the same!'

He wouldn't be consoled. He shoved past Esther and stormed to his room. When he came out, he pretended Haggis had never happened.

* * * *

Spring and summer came and went, and with it an almost hourly cycle of domestic victory and defeat. Esther just about managed to keep the score sheet even. Joshua grew several inches, absorbed some of Esther's inflections, some of Clyde's mannerisms. They were not necessarily the inflections and mannerisms his parents would have chosen to impart, but Esther and Clyde were prepared to look a gift horse square in the eye and say thank you. Somewhere along the line Joshua came to understand that conversation actually meant dialogue and, in deference to this new idea, he even learned to look like he was listening when other people spoke.

'Sometimes he's almost reasonable,' Esther told Clyde. 'I know it just seems that way. But at least he looks like he has some manners.' She frowned. 'Why does it feel like the only thing we've really taught him is camouflage and deceit?'

'Joshua's a pragmatist,' said Clyde with a grin. 'A little camouflage and deceit will take him a long way and I suspect he knows that.'

'Sometimes I have to steel myself for battle and challenge him just to prove I'm still in charge. Honestly, I never know whether to hug him or kill him. It's exhausting.'

'We'll get used to it. One of these days those walls of his will come tumbling down.'

'No they won't,' she said cheerfully.

* * * *

Joshua was home alone one evening. It was late summer, and the leaves hung drowsy and heavy with chlorophyll. He was in his room, moving the chair to catch the light, when he heard a sound at the back of the house.

'Esther?' he shouted, putting his head into the hall.

There was no answer, but a little later he heard it again — a scuffling noise.

Joshua was eminently practical. He knew ghosts to be an impossibility. He took a badminton racket from the front porch, closed and locked the back door, which had been wide open to the garden, and tracked the noise into Esther's study. The door was ajar and, as he pushed it open, he was stopped in his tracks by the astonishing sight of a book spontaneously falling out of the bottom shelf of the bookcase.

Joshua took a step backwards, his heart hammering. He flicked the study light on, off, on, off several times to steady himself, and when nothing further happened, he lifted the racket and advanced.

Sitting on the shelf where the book had been was a long, fat, spiky creature with a pointy nose and bright eyes.

'Haggis,' breathed Joshua. He put out both hands and the hedgehog happily walked straight onto them, wiggling his soft, vulnerable underbelly into Joshua's palms. Joshua held him for several minutes, crooning at him wordlessly. He didn't mind that the quills were sharp, that each small prick would later turn into an itchy red welt. It was Haggis. Haggis had come home.

Joshua fed him a saucer of milk and a couple of slugs from the garden. Then he took him outside, put him on the lawn, and went back inside. By the time Esther and Clyde came home, Haggis was gone.

'I wanted to keep him,' Joshua told them. 'I wanted to put him in the hedgehog house and close the door for the winter. But he's fat enough to hibernate and he has his own home somewhere.'

'He might even have a wife waiting for him,' suggested Esther.

Joshua gave her a withering look. 'He lives alone,' he informed her. 'In a warm brown hole with just a few leaves and a lot of food. I'll bet he's really happy.'

'Nice of him to let us know he was okay,' said Clyde.

Joshua rolled his eyes. 'Of course *he's* okay. He came back to check that we were okay.'

NEVER UNDERESTIMATE THE POWER OF A GOOD STORY

ALF HAYWOOD

BRIAN COULDN'T QUITE REMEMBER which of his friends first recommended Sue Loveton's latest novel to him; so many of them had drooled over it at the same time. 'They weren't wrong either,' he thought after reading a little of his special edition.

Later, on the train to London, he continued reading and found himself totally absorbed in the fictional lives of the characters. They flew off the pages with real problems, real situations and real heartaches. He was so involved in the story that his golden retriever needed to nudge him three times to indicate they were arriving at their destination.

In his haste to gather his rucksack and stick, the book escaped from his hand and slipped to the floor of the carriage. Fortunately there was, as usual, someone else there to rescue the situation. Three other passengers had all tried to retrieve the book for him but it was a woman — or a girl, he couldn't quite tell — who handed it back to him.

She tried to put it in his open hand but he moved towards her at the last second and it fell to the floor again. She became extremely flustered and apologised profusely as she scrambled to recover the book a second time.

'I'm so sorry, that was very clumsy of me but the book is fine. Just a little dustier than it was before.' She placed it much more carefully into the palm of his hand.

Too carefully really, as he briefly trapped one of her fingers. Brian apologised after that but was interrupted by other passengers anxious to leave the train.

'Can you manage the steps OK?' a concerned voice asked, as he started feeling for the platform with the toe of his shoe.

'I think so, but it's nice to know that someone cares enough to ask. It was you that handed me back that book I'm sure?'

She laughed lightly before replying, 'Yes it was. Is my voice that distinctive?'

'Everyone's voice is distinctive if you listen carefully. It's the best way to know who you are talking to. Male, female, young, old. It gives you the first clues to their personality and sometimes what they look like as well.'

'Surely you can't tell how someone looks just by hearing their voice?'

'Well not always. But I can make a fair stab at it. Want to know how I would describe you right now?'

'Only if you say something nice about me. I don't like being insulted by strangers.'

'I promise I won't insult you. If I do, I'll gladly buy you a cup of coffee and apologise.'

She laughed again but this time the sound was fuller and more relaxed. 'I think you've developed a rather unique chat-up line there. I bet it works with most of the girls you use it on.'

'I've never used it like this before. I suppose I need to find out if it works this time before I try it again.'

'It's working, take my word for it. Now tell me what I look like before I change my mind.'

'OK but maybe we should head for a coffee shop first in case I'm totally wrong.'

'I don't think you can do it. I was right all along about you pretending to be able to so that you can get a poor sucker like me to share a drink with you.'

Brian stopped walking towards the station exit and turned half-right towards some tables and chairs that had been set up outside a cafe. 'OK, I'll start but I might need a couple of tries because I think you're being a little careful about what you are saying. I think you are trying to distract me.'

'Stop making excuses and get on with it.'

'Here goes then. I'm guessing you're mid-thirties, kind of short, about five-two or three — with blue eyes. A bit of a country girl so probably wearing heavy tweedy-type clothes to hide the extra pounds and you keep your hair tied up in a bun on the back of your head — oh and brogue shoes, nothing fashionable.'

She burst out laughing long before he had finished but he already knew it was completely wrong. He reached out to guide her towards one of the tables and added, 'I'll tell you the real description over coffee. I still need a bit more information to complete the picture.'

Over coffee they talked about the novel he had been reading and why he liked it. She too knew the author and the story. During one lull in the conversation, and long after the empty coffee cups had gone cold, he looked slightly sideways at her face and began describing her.

'You're close to my height; about five-eight or nine because I can tell your mouth is just below mine. Mid-twenties like me and slim but not skinny because I felt your back as I guided you towards this table. You're wearing high heels that I can hear clearly as you walk along beside me. I also know you're wearing silk stockings because they make a particular sound and I heard that when you knelt down to pick up the book. Those stockings had to rub against a tight-fitting skirt and I know it's a skirt, not a dress, because when I touched your back, I also felt a belt. I don't know what colour your top is but I think it should be clean and bright like you are, so I'm going to say white. Am I doing any better this time?'

The girl hesitated before answering rather emotionally, 'Go on, I want to hear the rest.'

'Your hair is long and I think it just cascades over your shoulders because when you stood up to apologise I noticed your head turned rather quickly to both sides — I think you were trying to send your hair back behind you after it had fallen forward as you knelt down. I don't know what colour it is but your voice is calm and reassuring, not loud or attention-seeking like a redhead or natural blonde — probably mid-brown or auburn. When I caught your left hand finger on the train there was no wedding or engagement ring but I don't know if you have a boyfriend. I noticed the faintest whiff of perfume at the same time but it was more delicate than perfume, possibly eau de cologne; you neither want nor need to make strong statements about yourself. All those clues start to build a picture of someone who doesn't wear a lot of makeup, no eye shadow and just a light brush of delicate lipstick.

With all that going on around you, I think you would have to be quite beautiful with dark eyes. They could be green but you would look so much better if they were brown.'

Neither of them spoke after that for a few minutes. She was drinking in the description and he was desperate to hear her reaction.

After a long pause she reached out to stroke the back of his hand and murmured: 'Thank you.'

The waiter broke the silence by clearing cups and suggesting they should have a nice day. They both looked a little awkward as they stood up to leave and he covered his confusion by saying he was going to Moorfields eye hospital.

'I'm headed to a business meeting in the other direction.' After a pause, she asked: 'Why are you going to Moorfields?'

'One of the surgeons thinks he can operate to remove some bone that's squeezing the nerves between my brain and my eyes. If he's right, I should get my sight back in a month or two.'

'That would be fabulous for you. I'm sorry for delaying you with all that silly chatter. You must be dying to find out what he says.'

'I am, but if I ever see again I'll have to say goodbye to Beth here. She has been my eyes for so long now it will be like losing a part of me.'

'You'll have to start buying books all over again, real books with words rather than Braille ones. I really hope that surgeon has some good news for you.'

'I think he will. I'll probably be back here about three. I'll gladly wait to tell you what he says if you don't mind sharing another cup of coffee with me?'

'I'd like that.' She said picking up her bag. 'My meeting won't take that long but I don't mind waiting. I can always get a book to read.'

'That's great. I'll meet you here at three.' He held out his hand for hers. 'My name is Brian by the way. I don't think you gave me yours?'

'I didn't, it's Sue. Sue Loveton.' She called out as she walked away. She was in a hurry now; removing the blue contact lenses would be easy, but with only two months, how the hell could a blonde return to her natural mid-brown hair?

THE RUBY STRADIVARIUS

ISSY FLAMEL

SCRATCHING OF NIB ACROSS PAPER fills the room as Jacob prays for his hand to cease trembling and let him sign the contract. He closes his eyes and forces in a ragged breath, then screws the barrel of the pen back into its lid and places it with a solid clunk on the heavy mahogany of the table. He opens them to see a welcoming smile break across his new employer's face, the greying blond eyebrows arched above his cornflower-blue eyes.

'Congratulations Herr Shulman! And welcome to our little band.' He wraps Jacob's hand inside his and shakes it effusively.

'Thank you Herr Direktor, thank you! I hope, that is I know, I mean I want you to know…' The words come rushing out until the Direktor shushes him with a wave of his hands.

'Peace Jacob, peace, or how will you play? For, now we have the formalities over with, it is time.' As he speaks he leads them through a gleaming oak doorway. Jacob glides down a scarlet silk carpet under the opulent glint of gilded traceries and diamond sparkle of teardrop chandeliers, breathing in the history-heavy air, the echoes of ghostly applause showering down from the gods. And there it is. Balanced on a single chair, commanding the raked stage of the Konzerthaus, sits the Ruby Stradivarius, its dark, sinuous tones gleaming under the spotlight, throwing down its challenge.

'As leader it is yours, and only yours, to play as long as you are with us,' says the older man, and he gestures, inviting Jacob to claim his prize.

'I can't believe… all my life I've wanted… how did you come by such a masterpiece?' And instantly the question is regretted, as the first note of dissonance intrudes.

The esteemed Direktor pulls at his cuffs and shifts his glance away. Jacob feels, without being able to say why, that he has made a mistake, tarnished expectations, like the off-colour joke at a family funeral, or the unwanted advance that hangs in the air.

'We have been very fortunate, Herr Shulman. After the war, well, you know how things were. A generous benefactor, a reparation you might say.' He dabs his lips with a handkerchief and the words tail off.

Still Jacob stands, disturbed and dazzled by the moment, his limbs chained, until a controlling grip on his shoulder thrusts him forward. Now he cradles the violin in his hands, nestles it to his chin, and with a sweep of the bow it is singing, singing with such ethereal sweetness, rise after rise of spiralling cadenzas that flow one upon another as he feels the music pulse under his mastery, the strings shimmering. Plunged into ecstasy, Jacob is lost.

Until, in an instant, the polished instrument is now not ruby, but a roiling sea of blood, and the melody dies into a despairing, mournful glissando. Cold skeletal fingers entwine with his, falling whispers of ringlets brush his cheek and caress the living wood. Flesh pressing down on the strings, flesh pressing out against the razor-wire, a cremation ash of falling rosin gleaming under searchlights, as dogs snarl and the wail of the music is lost in a hellish rumble of wagon doors. Sing unto the Lord a new song. Hear me when I call, O God of my righteousness. Crimson flames glimmering in its curves, a defiant crescendo spills out, denying death, as a stolen life reclaims a stolen violin and sings its song into eternity.

American Style

William Webb

Sung to the tune of American Pie by Don McLean

A long, long time ago
I wrote prose
That made people smile
And I knew if I had an agent
They would treat me like a regent
All I had to do was send a file
But my submission made them shiver
With every query I'd deliver
Bad news slid down the mail ramp
I couldn't lick one more stamp
It's hard to think how hard I tried
How long I labored, laughed and sighed
But something snapped and broke my pride
The day the query died

So write, write with American Style
Got a laptop with a printer
'Cause the inkwells ran dry
And the folks in New York are reading maybe one line
Singin' add this piece of crap to the pile
Slush this one away in the pile

Did you write that book I read?
Can you raise it from the dead
If the agent buys your soul?
Do you believe it can really sell?

Can a contract relieve this living hell?
And can you teach me how to write really well?
Well you're addicted to the dream
Saw you typing last night about half past three
You worked until you cried
Man, I love the way you write
I was a college senior writing songs
With an old guitar and my roommate's bong
But I finally saw right from wrong
The day, the query died

So write, write with American Style
Got a laptop with a printer
'Cause the inkwells ran dry
And the folks in New York are reading maybe one line
Singin' add this piece of crap to the pile
Slush this one away in the pile

Now for ten years I've been writing alone
The local rag finally threw me a bone
But that's not how it used to be
When Adams hitchhiked in an English field
Drunk and broke, his fate seemed sealed
But his dream of fame refused to yield
And while the old man got lost at sea
Something wicked this way came to see
The way was paved with gold
All for Rowling alone to hold
And while agents read of a robot eye
And Gandalf caught him in the rye
We wrote stories of a sad goodbye
The day, the query died

We were typing —
Write, write with American Style
Got a laptop with a printer
'Cause the inkwells ran dry

AMERICAN STYLE

And the folks in New York are reading maybe one line
Singin' add this piece of crap to the pile
Slush this one away in the pile

The classics gather in a musty store cavern
The writers left for a darkened tavern
Sick and tired of playing the game
They drank and shouted that it's all the same
Can't get published it's a crying shame
And the newbie's in a corner thinking: fame
The tavern smelled of failed stale air
The patrons wondering why they were there
We all got up to leave
But we never got a reprieve
The cell phone rang a lonely tone
My agent made his intentions known
Do you recall what was atoned
The day, the query died

And we were drinking —
Write, write with American Style
Got a laptop with a printer
'Cause the inkwells ran dry
And the folks in New York are reading maybe one line
Singin' add this piece of crap to the pile
Slush this one away in the pile

And there we all were in one place
Writing lame copy in cyberspace
With no will left to try again
So come on Dan be nimble Dan be quick
Dan Brown's on the best seller list
'Cause conspiracy is what we all insist
We paid to see his story staged
Debated words he put on the page
Yet no editor born today
Would let me write that way

The Best of Writerlot

And as sales climbed high and advances soared
I threw myself upon Tolkien's sword
The agent laughing at my words
The day, the query died

The agent was singing —
Write, write with American Style
Got a laptop with a printer
'Cause the inkwells ran dry
And the folks in New York are reading maybe one line
Singin' add this piece of crap to the pile
Slush this one away in the pile

I met a girl I'd like to thank
Whose grass was greener on her septic tank
But she just said she's At Wit's End
So I went online to the new book store
Where I heard we writers had a chance to score
But the BookSurge said I had to pay
And in the Twilight the young ones screamed
The authors cried they were getting creamed
Not a contract was written
The agents all were smitten
By the three queries they admired most
Wizards, vamps, and the celebrity roast
So they traded the writer for a ghost
The day, the query died

And we were tweeting —
Write, write with American Style
Got a laptop with a printer
'Cause the inkwells ran dry
And the folks in New York are reading maybe one line
Singin' add this piece of crap to the pile
Slush this one away in the pile.

Rebel Rebel

Gary Bonn

'SO, IT'S 11:00 PM HERE IN FROSTY GLASGOW. Over the next few hours the temperature will drop to -11, and everyone is talking about the cut in winter fuel supplements for the elderly.' Siobhan pauses for breath, flicks long black from hair from her headset and pushes on. 'I'm opening the lines now. You know the number and you know me. Don't phone with wet opinions; I want facts, who's being affected and how. I mean, the cuts make sense, all the elderly will die off so the government don't have to pay their pensions and they get a nice trickle of inheritance tax to pay for their love nests. Welcome to The Combat Zone.'

Two buttons pressed and she announces, 'This is Immolate from Sighthill. Three minutes of glorious Glasgow rock.'

She sits back, sips water. Blue lipstick on a plastic cup. Tapping a blue fingernail against a tooth, she waits for the call lights to come on. Nothing. Stupid producers, who is going to phone about this at this time? Wankers. The city is crawling with drugs and prostitutes right now, and she has to talk about…

Wait. A call.

'I'm interrupting Immolate for our first call. Hello, whoever you are. What's up?'

A breathless, rushed voice. The rattle of coins in a callbox. 'Siobhan, it's me, Connel Roxburgh. I need to tell you something…'

'Connel, I don't take personal calls on air. This had better be about…'

'Siobhan, I'm going to die. Listen to me.'

'Call an ambulance!'

'No, someone's going to kill me.'

'Connel, call the police.' Siobhan breathes an inner sigh of relief. Connel may have been the weedy nerd, bullied right up to sixth form, a spotty, lanky-haired misfit, but at least what he's saying will wake up her dwindling audience.

'Like the police could do anything.'

'What...?'

'Siobhan, listen. I was invited to a meeting. I thought it was to be a social thing, but it was a Rebel cell. They wanted to enroll me. Told me what an asset I'd be. I think they just saw me as a pushover. My initiation was to kill a man in Govan, some guy in Hislop Road. They gave me a gun and told me to be back in two hours.'

'Is this some sort of joke? Because...'

'Listen, they probably guessed I wouldn't do it. They followed me, but I dodged them at Queens Street station. Half the Rebels in the world will be out looking for me now.'

'Connel, get out. Get to a police station or something.' Siobhan feels Connel's pressure of speech, the jagged breath and desperation in his words pulling her in.

'What's the point? If they don't get me today, it'll be tomorrow. I'm a dead man. Look, Siobhan, I've got something to say. I'm sick of all this killing. The papers tell us it's about the Rebels and the State. That's bollocks. This is all about violent bastards screwing scared people. It's all based on old prejudices that no one gives a toss about any more. It's done for power, the buzz and the money the bastards get from intimidation.'

'Connel...'

'Look, it's obvious. The criminals, the murderers at the top will kill their own kind if they stand up to them. They don't really care if you are one of them, the police or the army. All they want is wealth and power. Out there, all over the place, are good, kind people that don't care about ancient history, don't want the violence to go on, don't want to get pulled in.' He pauses. 'Shit, a car just went past. People looking out at me.'

'Connel, please run!'

'No chance. It's stopping.'

Siobhan juts two fingers at her director and waves a fist. Behind glass, he's making gestures like he wants her to cut the conversation.

'Connel, my boss wants me to cut you off. I swear to God, if he touches the connection, I'll kill him. Go on.'

'If all these perverted bastards knew how many people are against them. Hey, if everyone wore a red badge, you know, like they are sick of blood. No! If everyone wore a red badge with the names of all the family or friends they've lost, we'd all see just how evil these people are and how much we all hurt because of their greed. Maybe... Fuck, two have got out. It must be them.'

Siobhan's words tumble out before she's aware of them. 'You've got a gun, kill them!'

'I don't kill people, Siobhan. Look, this has been going on for years. The graveyards are full of mums, dads, children... The body count rises nearly every day. Why do people listen to idiots who think the only way you can solve a problem is by making it worse? Here they come. Hey, Siobhan, it's been lovely talking to you. Do you know how many times I tried to at school? My tongue seized up every time. It was like you're some sort of princess and I was just...'

'Connel!' Siobhan shrieks as two shots ring out. Glass smashes, the receiver clatters against something hard. Gasps and groans from Connel. The sound of a door opening is followed by two clearer, louder shots. The door slams on silence.

Siobhan screams. Tears run. She's shaking, spluttering. 'Oh, dear God, dear God...' Draws a sleeve across the mucous running from her nose.

'Connel, oh, God, Connel.' She takes a shuddering breath in. She's not aware of the time passing, just rocking back and forth, moaning and snivelling. 'Bastards... bastards. Is there no end to this *fucking* stupidity?'

A thought rises and hammers into consciousness — she's still on air. 'Listeners, a man just died. Died giving us a message. I've got a red cup-mat here. I'm sticking a safety pin through it and writing "Connel Roxburgh" on it. Tell everyone you know.'

WORKING IT OUT

LOUISE COLE

SEAN MACKS WAS ONCE THE LOVE of someone's life. It may seem remarkable to us now, that this man, cursed with relentless adolescence, who couldn't even raise the energy to trim a rampant privet hedge, had inspired such passion in anyone but his mother.

'Huh?' said Sean Macks. 'That's not fair. The hedge wasn't rampant. It was bushy.'

You see, a woman had built her world around him and, in retrospect, she thought the hedge story summed him up rather well. She had listened in dismay to his elderly neighbours' argument that the rampant shrubbery left only three feet of pavement, which wasn't nearly enough for two zimmer frames to clunk along side by side through the final days of their marriage. Macks' girlfriend, Lucy, thought it rather beautiful that they still wanted to hobble along side by side.

Macks chose to defend the hedge's right to grow as nature intended.

He refused to cut the hedge until the very morning the council contractors were despatched to slice it down for him. He beat them to the buzz of the chainsaw by mere minutes, proving to himself that his soul was still as anarchic as when he was sixteen. In fact, the only difference between his youthful Marxist spirit and his 30-something soul was circumstance. That is to say, Macks now owned a considerable number of possessions, including a small terraced house. After all, if property is theft, one may as well be an anarchic thief as a homeless anarchist.

'Piss off,' said Sean Macks. 'That's the most insulting thing I've ever heard.'

However, it is hard to believe that, following a life of wasted talent and missed opportunity such as Macks', this assertion is even remotely true.

'Oi, what's going on? What have I ever done to you?' Macks was infuriated. *'You can't just reduce someone's life to a few throwaway lines. This is defamatory.'*

It isn't defamatory, however, to recall the day when his mother had insisted on his bringing Lucy home for dinner. He had obliged, of course, seating his pregnant girlfriend at the table and solicitously piling her plate with roast meat and veg. Catering for her every need, in fact, except her very necessary defence against his mother.

'So when are you two marrying?'

Lucy forced a small smile toward her curled, crispy vegetables. Mrs Macks didn't consider anything cooked unless its soul had been purified by fire.

'Not now, Mum,' said Sean. 'We're eating.'

But Mrs Macks wasn't of a generation which considered talk of marriage should put a real man off his food.

'Well, hasn't he asked you then?' she persisted, topping up Lucy's tea. Tea, with dinner. Doesn't that tell you everything you need to know?

(No, it bloody doesn't, you nasty little snob. You leave my mum alone. She's a good person.)

(Hey. Let me out.)

Indeed, one would hope she is a better person than her son, who didn't respond to her latest sally and left his girlfriend to stab at her meat, eyes down. His mother sailed on like a Spanish galleon, all ignorance and flamboyance in the face of imminent defeat.

'Well, don't you want to get married, Lucy? You must think of the baby, you know.'

Lucy put down her fork carefully. So carefully, in fact, that anyone with even a lemming's sense of self-preservation would have left the room swiftly and silently. But the Macks family were inured against subtlety in the way politicians are inured to conscience. It had been bred out of them over many generations.

'I have asked *him*,' she said, very softly. 'He doesn't want to marry me.' Her gaze snapped onto the older woman like an industrial magnet onto a steel girder. 'Alright?'

'I… well…' Mrs Macks stumbled for a second. Could it be true that the man in front of her, the boy she had raised, would get a girl in trouble and then abandon her? Not stand by her? For a second, her whole world swung dizzyingly.

(But there you are, you see. Look at that language. Abandonment. Trouble. What century do you think this is? Do you really believe those terms apply to a woman today? This is not a balanced account. It's inflammatory. You publish any of this and I'll call a lawyer.)

Sean Macks doesn't have a lawyer. Anarchists, of course, tend not to.

Anyway, back to the old matriarch. It could be worse, she thought. At least my husband isn't alive to see his only son behave so dishonourably.

(Oh please, this is just twisted. Not only would nothing in this world make my mother glad that her husband was dead but, actually, that wasn't what upset her. Then or now. You may be the narrator but you are not omniscient. In fact, I don't think you know your characters at all.

My mother was upset because if I wasn't married and Lucy decided to leave me, I would have no rights to my son. No rights as an unmarried father. How prescient was that, eh? My mother was looking out for me and my kid. Children need their Dads. You tell Lucy that. From me.)

Enough! I am telling this story. You are my character.

(I am Sean Macks. I am no one's character.)

You are not Sean Macks. You are just a ghost of Sean Macks. An echo, caught in this page. Even Sean Macks is just a ghost of who he used to be.

(So you admit I'm real then?)

Not you. You are nothing. Just an empty voice. Words on a page. But the real Sean Macks. Yes. He's out there.

(How did you drag me here then? Where am I? I mean out there, where am I? I need to go.)

(And stop doing that.)

Stop doing what?

(Wrapping these fences around me so I can't get out. Let me go.)

Fences? Oh, you mean the parentheses? That's brackets to you, Sean. I'm not going to let you go. If I let you loose, you'll take over. The way you took over...

Anyway. Let's return to young Lucy. She had her baby and Sean stood by her. At least he stood by the bed and squinted through half-shut eyes as she strained and screamed, her fingers twisting and pinching his reddened skin.

As he saw his son born, love hit Sean Macks like a God-given epiphany. He hadn't known what he had been missing. The pride, the sense of accomplishment, the moment of realisation that he had done it. If he died tomorrow, this child was his mark on the face of the universe, his signature across the heavens. He told Lucy she hadn't done badly, all things considered, kissed his kid and went to the pub to reflect on the meaning of parenthood.

(Oh that's just not fair…)

Shut UP!

Sean Macks wasn't a bad Dad. He loved his son because of how it made him feel to be a father. He loved his girlfriend because she had played a role in giving him a son. To Sean Macks, this was the beautiful symmetry of life in a nutshell.

He talked about his son all the time. When he was at work, when he was out with his friends, and, often, to Lucy, in the brief interludes between getting in from work and going out with his friends.

(When did she talk to me? About anything but our boy I mean? They were like a little club, the two of them, and I wasn't a member.)

He provided — with some difficulty because it's hard to reconcile earning a very large salary with anarchism and, in particular, with a refusal to work long hours — for them both and assumed, in his folly, that Lucy and his child had all they needed.

Until he came home one day and found them gone.

(*)

Don't you dare start putting footnotes in the text. I was a bloody footnote. For so long, Sean. Living in the margins of *your* life.

(Lucy?)

How could you just ignore us, Sean? How could you bloody ignore us?

(I didn't. I didn't mean to. I need you, baby.)

It's all about you isn't it? Everything becomes about you.

(Just… look, let me out of here, will you? Let me talk to you.)

But Lucy knew, in her heart, it was too late. The die had been cast, the ship had sailed, the arrow had left the —

(Just stop it. STOP IT LUCE. Stop this narrator crap. You want to dictate your life, that's fine. Why didn't you?

What?

Why bloody didn't you? If you were so desperate to be the writer of your own book, why did you sit on a settee and weep because I wasn't there? Why didn't you get up and start living your own life?

Lucy?

You're out. How did you get out?
Fat tears burned hot on Lucy's cheeks, smudging her words.
I won't hurt you. I was angry, that's all. I guess you can bust through lots of fences when you're angry enough. Listen, Lucy, just talk to me. I promise, I won't ask anything of either of you. Just talk to me.
Why?
Because I love you. I've always loved you.
I don't know where you are.
Sean Macks smiled and wiped a smear of ink from Lucy's cheek. 'Yeah, you do. I'm in your head and in your heart. I'm even in your writing. What else do you need to know?'

Lucy leaned over the buggy next to her. 'What do you think sweetie? Should we go see Daddy?'

The baby smiled indiscriminately, as babies do.

Lucy let the pen drop from her fingers and reached for her coat.

* I was devastated. No note. Nothing.

Umwelt: When It's Time to Party...

Ren Warom

EEP, DISTORTED THUMP OF MUSIC. Heavy beats underlie a dissonant slew of synth. Heads bob up, down, human pistons in the dance machine. Hair flies like a multitude of wings: blonde, red, black, purple, blue. Arms wave dry fog to swirls of intricate eddies, pictograms of movement.

Through undulating torsos, scantily clad tits, hips, slick with sweat, we enter the eye of the limb hurricane. She dances there alone, magnificent, careless. Dress a sparkling purple scrap, hair wild, eyes closed and layered with green glitter-shadow, stark black Egyptian kohl.

Bright lips, blood red, stretch a smile of sheer bliss. Arms sway in slow, feline movements. A hand reaches from fog, grasps her wrist and Margo's eyes snap open; her predatory red mouth beams delight. She bolts forward, leaps, and wraps limbs around Rolf like tentacles.

Yells in his ear, 'About fucking time. I need a fag, twenty million more White Russians and a piss.'

Rolf giggles as she unpeels. Hooks his arm through hers. They slice through the crowd. Margo's elbows are battering rams. Half-naked whores pitch off cheap heels to sprawl, ape-like and undignified, on the floor.

One downed blonde screams, 'Bitch!' She's laid there, spread-eagled. Knickers exposed. French silk. Drooling men stare, bug-eyed.

'So clumsy,' Margo drawls, teeth exposed, hyena cruel. 'Perhaps invest in orthopaedic clogs?'

'Fuck me clogs!' shouts Rolf, and collapses to giggles.

Margo grins, a dirty leer. Her eyes pop. 'Oooh. Speaking of fuck me clogs...' Long, prehensile fingers grasp his jaw, pull and stroke.

'Where's that five o'clock fuck me shadow?'

'Darling, it was more euthanise me than fuck me…'

Margo snorts laughter. Struts. Shimmies. Rolf minces alongside; tight arse wiggling in spray-on-leather as they hit the bar. Margo slams down a hand tipped with hooked, black claws.

'Alcohol, at once!'

* * * *

Margo squats beside a dumpster. Thin trickles of piss wind out between the pointy toes of her sparkling shoes. They slow. Stop. Margo stands. With one hand she yanks knickers up, dress down. The other clutches a glass filled with creamy white alcohol and a long black cigarette.

She flicks ash, slugs her White Russian. Rolf leans forward, zipping up, leaving piss steaming on the wall.

'Where the fuck is Moe?'

Margo leaps to the dumpster edge. Her legs dangle, akimbo. One heel, half off, swings. Diamante flashes yellow reflections from street lamps.

'Stood me up, the dirty cunt. Not the first time. He'll turn up.'

Rolf pouts. 'Oh! When? Did I waste my tightest tighty-whiteys?'

Margo slugs, shrugs, careless. 'Fashionably late?'

'Bollock off, sweets.' Rolf hops up. Snatches the fag. Drags long and deep. Declares, 'I'm fashionably fucking late. Moe's practically erstwhile.'

Margo hiccups. Holds up bare wrists. 'Not on the clock, wouldn't know.'

Rolf sniffs. Mutters, 'Never known you to be off the cock.' Thrusts his wrist out. A giant gold Rolex dazzles.

Margo peers at the face. She squints, blinks, glances at Rolf and then back at the watch. Wobbles. Looks off down the alley, bottom lip clamped in sharp little teeth.

'Shit.'

Rolf nods. Emphatic. 'Precisely, my big breasted bitch. He's overdue.'

'Darling,' Margo announces, 'if he were my period, I'd be in the bathroom with a hanger.'

She huffs, thrusts out her tits, mulish. Her free hand digs into Rolf's pocket, grabs at various bulges. He jumps, yelps as Margo pulls out a slim gold phone. Rolf clutches his dick, whimpers. She pinches it. Vicious. Laughs like a drain.

'Poof.'

He shoves her. 'Slag.'

'Anal jizz spurt.'

'Rotten cunt cheese.'

They lock eyes. Giggle. Margo dials. Listens, then screeches, 'Fuckin' ansaphone.' She waits a moment and then unleashes full drama mode. 'Moe. I'm liver-deep in White Russians, up to my lungs in fags. And where are you? In absentia. Treason! Rolf's here and I can tell you darling, his arse is tighter than a Bishop's nostril.' A filthy, inebriated grin smears across her face. 'Imagine it, Moe, like skull fucking an anus.'

Rolf shrieks, grabs for the phone. They wrestle. Tussle. Margo falls back, howling. Rolf rolls her over. Smack her arse hard. Once. Twice. And again. She wiggles it, half hanging off the dumpster. Looks over her shoulder, her eyes wicked smoke.

'Mmm. Tasty.' Margo pushes up peering down at the filthy tarmac. There's a puddle of alcohol beside the dumpster, cloudy as spunk, shot through with glass shards. Margo pouts. 'You knocked my fucking drink.'

'So let's buy a fuckin' nother,' he sneers, grabs her arse, leaps off the dumpster. Margo screams, delighted. Hangs down his back. Her teeth lock on tasty tight arse cheek.

'Ach, bitch, get off.'

A cooing call echoes down the alley. Margo rises up, hands on Rolf's arse for balance. Screams in delight, 'My best bitch.' Margo tugs Rolf's jeans. 'Giddy up homo!'

Rolf drops her down, shrieking giggles. Hauls her up, legs either side of his neck and sets off down the alley. Margo shoves her head through his legs. Grins.

'Look, backwards sixty-nine!'

He chokes. Holds her ankles in one hand and uses the other to push her back through. 'Men only,' he shouts and runs off, bouncing her, because he knows she loves it.

Halfway down they meet miniature pre-Raph Minnie tottering along on spiky black heels. She's wrapped in yellow PVC, tits pumped to max exposure, and her nipples flash as she moves.

'Cunt and centre you two.' Minnie shimmers. The air behind her bends, re-shapes to tall gothic arches, fluttering feathers. There, then gone. 'I had one of my moments. Moe's hit a snag on the razz. Leek's already there with him, I sent her ahead with my new boy toy, Slimm.'

Margo grabs Rolf's knees. Yanks. Sticks her head between. 'What's the snag?'

'Ravids. So shake a tail feather.'

Margo flips. Lands feet down behind Rolf. Leans a chin on his shoulder. 'You've got the feathers, bitch.'

Minnie grins. 'So shake your fucking tits, then.'

'That,' says Margo, 'I can fucking do.'

* * * *

The sound of howling, baying Ravids carries on the air. Margo struts on, click clack. Her glittering purple dress fades out, fades in. Silver gleams in its stead, sculpted tight to her heart-shaped arse. Bronze holds breasts in scrolling loops, just contained. Ripe. Erotic.

Minnie lands, her wings send a rough breeze to ruffle Margo's magenta locks. 'Ready?'

Margo's sword sings from its sheath. 'Oh, hell yes.'

Two long whips crack out, corded black leather, their ends solid links of etched steel. They crack again, fold to loops in Rolf's hands. He's half-naked. Glorious. His alabaster perfection of features continues to a torso rippled as a statue, his periwinkle-blue eyes reflect Margo's katana blade.

'Oh, bitch, I love it when you fight dirty.'

She smiles long, lewd, a murderous bitch about to party. Struts alongside. They move to easy lope, the soft whoosh of wind from Minnie's wings rifling their hair. Dive headlong toward the mess up ahead.

In the decrepit innards of an old store yard, their backs to the wall, Moe, Leek, and a tall, fox-eyed stranger, slash, cut and slice against a raving horde. Send gouts of blood, like banners, to colour walls, floor, faces in festive red. Before them, the mob is fifty strong and waning. Ravids. Mechanised revenants. Dead eyes, rotted flesh, machine innards gleaming solid metal. Hard to kill. Minnie swoops to land, face lit in a dazzled smile. She points to the fox-eyed stranger.

'That delicious creature is Slimm. He fucks like a goddamn Brazilian man-whore.'

'The fuck?' Margo breathes, eyes agleam.

'Mine,' Minnie hisses, claws up, at full length. Six-inch long scythes glint in the moonlight, the hazy glow of streetlamps.

Margo pivots. Her katana sweeps down, a delicate arc. Ravid arms fly up, like confetti. Pretty. They hit the ground in a mixture of meaty thunks and metallic sparks, clinks. 'All yours, darling,' Margo says to Minnie, batting her eyelashes. 'Far too tall.'

The sound of Rolf's whips cut the air. Ravid heads sail overhead, out of the yard walls. His torso is spattered red, ebony hair tousled, dripping sanguine showers. It trickles down his face, blood tears, and he yells to Leek over the sea of Ravids, 'Who sent them?'

Leek, tall as Slimm, slender as willow, head to toe in black straps, her skin showing in pearl white stripes, looks up. Grins. Shouts, 'Don't know. Could be anyone. Can you reach for it?'

'Too many. Need to kill at least half, buy me some time.'

'Need to slice and dice,' she screams back. 'These are expensive, they won't fucking stop till nothing's left.'

Sure enough, a scrape of noise comes from behind and Rolf turns. Three headless Ravids reach for him, brutal, strong, mindless with fury. He yelps. Leaps back. Cracks his whips out like bullets, twists them to balletic tornado and churns the Ravids to a slippery metal flesh pile. The stench of putrid innards hits like a bulldozer. He coughs. Spits. Turns to Margo, Minnie. Yells, 'When it's time to party…'

Margo whoops, screams, 'We'll party hard motherfucker.'

Minnie dives. Scoops one Ravid in iridescent black wings. Corkscrews, and lets it loose. Tosses it straight at Moe. Slender piratical Moe, all muscles and eyes like chocolate. Delicious. Midair, the Ravid lets out a strange, mewling cry.

Moe's face, rakish perfect, tilts to the heavens. 'Incoming!' he roars.

A storm of wings blows in, black as Minnie's. As they wheel down, black reveals as inky, liquid occult haze. Flickers like a hologram. Wings, feathers and then only skeletal, eyeless crows. They boil, a tornado of bones. Minnie snaps back her wings. Her face becomes a feral snarl. Those nail-scythes rise and a bloodcurdling scream leaves luscious pink lips. She attacks.

Below, Margo and Rolf fight back to back, a human blender,

purifying Ravids. Leave only a chunky, liquid mass of parts and twisted metals as they go. His whips move, sinuous power, her katana creates an endless song of slicing steel, atom suicide, ring and spark, as a rain of delicate bones begins to fall.

They hit the wall. Grins pass between blood-drenched faces. Ravids down to twenty. Less. Rolf laughs. Margo elbows Moe. Her grin suggestive, dirty. He rolls those chocolate-drop eyes. Pinches her tit. Carries on slaying.

Calls to Rolf without looking, 'Leek says you can read these. So read.'

Rolf nods, eyes wide as saucers on Moe and tries not to drool. He cracks his whips to coils, reaches out to snag a Ravid. This one's armless, missing chunks of torso. Machinery sputters sparks in the holes. It's weak but struggles to reach muscled flesh, teeth metal spines sharp as a barracuda's.

Rolf holds it down. Places a hand over the nose, the rolling red eyes. His eyelids shutter periwinkle blue and his mind leaps inside dead thoughts. Flies trapped in amber. It's cold in there, black, mindless. He shivers, flesh contracting to goosebumps, but plunges further past freezing emptiness to recorded memory. It's like diving an endless tunnel of thick, icy water.

Then. There. Foggy distance springs to full technicolour, and he sees. Starts to talk, voice a flat monotone, 'Men. Seven. No, nine. Suits. They conjure. Call the Ravids. Rare, expensive ingredients. They're pleased. These will be unbeatable. Small band will not become coherent whole. A problem solved.'

Margo leans over, and Katana punches through the chest of a pouncing Ravid as she goes. She licks his ear, croons, 'Who are they?'

Rolf's head tilts, his eyes leap open. Blue has bled to black, corner to corner. Margo sees her face reflected. Shudders. He's so beautiful. His mouth opens. 'Order,' he intones. 'Order of nine.'

'Where do we need to go?'

Rolf twitches, his black gaze glows. He follows in further. Slices through the memory of Ravid summons and jumps into the ghostly minds of the Order. It's dangerous, he could lose himself in here, but it's vital. Further, deeper, he pushes, relentless. Sifts memories like sand.

There. He stops at the memory of a closed meeting. Only two members of the Order are present. Orders are being given to four suited men. Walls of heavy muscle, blank faced in shades, with huge guns strapped to their hips.

'Find the Angel,' he moans to Margo. 'Stop Mother Immortal.'

Margo signals to Moe, Leek, Minnie, Slimm. 'He's found it.'

'Can he take us?' Leek, busy with two Ravids. Her blades, flashing bright as diamonds, send fountains of blood and machine fluid spurting into the night.

Margo shakes her head. 'We'll have to take ourselves. He can show us the way though.'

'Then let's fucking do this.'

Margo leans back to Rolf. 'Show us the way, baby. Show us where they went.'

Rolf jumps to the four. Follows where they go. A hot, desert planet. Double suns. One leprous yellow, blinding bright. The other leering red. Alive. Malevolent. He sends the image back down the line, through Margo's soft lips on his ear, to five eager minds.

They gather the worlds to them, knife through, fold from here to there. Six beautiful, bedraggled bodies blur, fade to shadow. Disappear. Eight Ravids, all that's left, raise ravaged heads: roar their fury to the winds.

The remains of the bone crow storm swoops down, descends upon the last Ravids, and a plague of tearing beaks strip them to heaps of tangled bone and machine parts glinting on gore-drenched concrete. Puddles of blood and machine fluids steam into the cool air as the crow cloud rises, funnels off into starless dark, their caws mournful as lost souls.

Party's over…

More *Umwelt* is available at **www.writerlot.net**

A BOY IN GRAY

BILL 'BOOPADOO' SAUER

A letter, found on the dressing table of eight-year-old Charlotte Rae Beaumont of Charleston, South Carolina.

28 March, 1863

Dearest Charlotte,

It is with no lack of sadness I write this letter to you. I am sorry to leave you so, to pull feet under cover of night like this, but I have a call to answer. Today begins my fifteenth year upon creation, and I am man enough now that I must do my duty, as Papa did before me. I am off to see the elephant. I shall go across lots to reach General Lee's Army of Northern Virginia, with whom I fully intend to enlist and wage battle against the Yankee aggressors who took our papa away from us. Surely they will accept my application. I am already the best shot in four counties.

Do not be sad for me, dear sister. Though the Federals deserved righteously to be so catawamptiously chewed up by General Lee's boys after taking our papa at Fredericksburg, it is up to me to avenge him right proper. Rufus, had he lived past the age I am today, would do the same in my place, but he did not and so must I.

Mama will need you to be strong for her. She has lost a son and a husband, and surely she will be of mind to think I will be lost as well, but you must keep her spirits up! You must convince her I am in earnest as I promise you both: I shall be back when all this unpleasantness is through. I will be giving you both great big bear hugs in no time at all.

Charlotte, you must mind Mr Tolliver from now on. As property boss, he is the closest you and Mama have to a man of the house in my stead. He will protect you both, of that I am sure. Mind him as if he were me, or even Papa, and mind Mama as well. She and Miss Bonnie will need your help running the house. No more tricks and pranks on Miss Bonnie from now on. I know you would promise me this to my picture if you could, so I will let you in on a secret. Under the third floorboard from the eastern rail of the rear porch off the kitchen you will find my stash of molasses candy. It is yours now. I shall not be needing such things of childhood in Virginia.

Chin up, dear sister, I'll not be gone for long. If Fredericksburg has been an indicator of things to come, we'll be chasing those Federals out of Dixie in no time, for good and all proper. I have written another letter to Mama, so that you may keep this one between you and I, a special goodbye for my baby sister. Until I have opportunity to hug you again, I remain faithfully and lovingly your big brother,

Tobias

More of *A Boy in Gray* is available at **www.writerlot.net**

TRAIN IN VAIN

PATRICK LECLERC

I'D NEVER REALLY LIKED ABBY. Not since she started seeing John. I mean, I had known him for years and it felt like she stole him from me. Not that I'd ever actually told him how I felt, but it was always there. I mean, I had been there for him before he got his first gig, before he managed to cobble his high school buddies together into a band, through it all.

John met Abby at a show, one of his early ones, back when the band was playing tiny, smoky venues whose patrons largely ignore the acts and where you stuck to the floor in the bathroom, if you were brave enough to venture in. She was his first big fan. Well, after me, but his first big fan who hadn't known him before.

I'd originally pegged her as the usual groupie slut, but that's unfair. For one, the band wasn't big enough to justify groupie sluts, certainly not ones as attractive as she was, and she did seem to actually want to spend time with John in general, not just at shows.

In the beginning, she was good for him. Even I, looking at the situation through my too green eyes, had to admit that. She pushed him to try new things, took him to see sights, made him experience things. That's what she always called it. Experiencing. She never just *did* anything. For his part, he seemed to flourish with her. At first. He had more energy, he took more interest in life, he was actually more fun to be around. And his music got better.

He went from garage band with potential to the darling of the Boston underground rock scene. His normal lack of ambition fell away. I'd given up trying to get him to promote his work, or even to put the time in. He'd always give me the spiel about "needing to be inspired". I would just grind my teeth in frustration as my work on posters, websites and hours spent trying to hawk his CDs at indie record stores went ignored or unappreciated.

But when she came into the picture, he changed. He cared. He wrote songs non-stop. He actually talked to record store owners. He stayed after shows and talked to his fans, who finally started to merit the plural version of the noun.

She was subtle. Pushing him and pulling alternately. She could have written a book on carrot and stick motivation, because he never felt manipulated. Even I had a hard time seeing it, and I was looking. I wanted to find a flaw, to see an evil plot behind her actions, but for a long time I couldn't. Even when I did see the way she worked her magic on him, the subtle hints, the changes in attitude that made him want to impress her without her needing to say a word, I couldn't expose her and cast her out. She was jut pushing him the way I wished I could. The times I found her cold and bitchy, cruel far beyond my own limits with him, the result on his drive was exactly what I had been trying to achieve for years.

The difference was that my pushing was dismissed as nagging, and made him obstinate. Her merest expression of disappointment was like a cattle prod forcing him to action. And she was wild and fun and uninhibited enough that the positive reinforcement she handed out obviously ensured that he tried for more. I still didn't like her, but I could see she was good for him, and that she was what he needed. I even enjoyed being around him more when she was around. He was more animated, more alive. I shoved my jealousy down and just told myself that he was happy, that's what mattered. I needed to accept that he and I was something that simply wasn't going to happen.

And for two years, that's exactly what I did. Through the band's climb to semi-respectability and an actual real, honest-to-God offer from an, albeit small, label. They sounded good, polished and real. He was happy, the rest of the band were content, and I was resigned.

But Abby wasn't happy.

She cooled towards John and the band. Subtly at first, then more noticeably. Her praise was cutting in its mediocrity. A lukewarm compliment from her hurt him more than the most outrageous trashing by any other critic and she knew it. Yet she still did it, even though the band was getting better venues, making money and playing with more technical skill that ever. The heap of CDs in her car never seemed to include his latest work, and progressively less of his older stuff. Every t shirt she wore flaunting other bands seemed calculated to twist a knife in him at a time when he should be riding high on his success.

Tonight was the last straw. I came by to help him with some updates to the website, and the promotional stuff for the latest shows. I found him sitting in a daze, looking for all the world like he'd been hit with a two-by-four.

'What's wrong?' I asked. He was white as a ghost.

'She's banging Tom,' he muttered. At least that's what it sounded like.

'Who's whating whom?' I demanded.

He turned to face me, his eyes fixed on some horribly painful sight far, far away. The look you only see in photos of refugees and soldiers who've been to hell. I stepped back. I'd never actually seen that look on someone I knew.

'Abby. My girlfriend. Is banging. Tom. My fucking A&R guy!' The sentence started out as a flat whisper and ended as a tortured roar, full of more rage and pain that I thought could exist.

'Oh my God,' I stammered. 'I'm so sorry. Is there anything I can do?'

He shook his head. He shook himself. 'I need to get it out of my system.'

I opened my mouth to assure him how willing I was to listen, but he cut me off, standing abruptly and seizing his guitar. 'I'm sorry. I just need some time with my guitar. The only one who's never deserted me.'

I was hurt. Yes, it was melodramatic, spoken in a moment of pain, but it still cut deep. I had always been there. To listen, to help, to support. Maybe I never sucked his dick behind a stack of amps between sets, but I never deserted him either.

I left the apartment numb, but I didn't stay that way long. A rage flared up in me. How dare she toss him aside like that? For some dirtbag suit? I didn't even remotely understand it. If she was into money and power, why had she dated a musician in the first place?

Well, she wasn't getting away with it. Of that I was certain. What I planned to do I didn't know, but it would be something, dammit.

It took me two days to track down Abby's apartment. During that time, John had been buried in the studio, venting his fury in verse. He angrily dismissed Tom, and delivered such a blistering rant to the label that they had to grovel and offer him a lot of control on the next album to keep him from walking out the door. Or tossing the next A&R guy out of a window. It was a close thing.

Her apartment was in an older building in Allston, off Harvard Ave. The kind rented by college students, artists, musicians, and apparently cheap, cheating skanks. I paused at the buzzer before trying it. Why should she let me in? I knew she was home, I could see light in her window and watched her silhouette pass back and forth a few times.

As I stood wondering what to do, my knight in shining armor appeared in the form of a Chinese take-out delivery boy. As he mounted the steps, I fumbled in my purse cursing about lost keys. When he was buzzed it, he held the door for me with a polite bow. I smiled and thanked him. I did look like I belonged in this neighborhood, and didn't seem like a murderer or a burglar, so I don't think his actions were really of any concern to anybody but the most anal, security-obsessed paranoid, and that type simply didn't live on this side of town. I walked past the handful of bicycles in the hallway, ignored the marijuana plant on the windowsill and climbed the old curving Victorian stairs with the wide, sweeping banister, past a mural of angels and demons that some budding Michelangelo had done in tempera paint.

I stopped in front of Abby's door, and took a deep breath. I was about to knock when I heard a voice.

'Come in, Kate.'

I pushed the door open and stepped into the apartment. It was a shrine to rock and roll. Posters and band announcements covered the walls, albums, tapes and CDs covered every flat surface in drunkenly-leaning stacks. Her collection would be the envy of every music snob who ever said, 'I only like their early stuff'. For instance, I spotted a copy of London Calling, but not Combat Rock. Born to Run but not Born in the USA. No "Greatest Hits" albums from anybody. Most of it was on vinyl, and most was rock, but there was a smattering of classical music and the odd blues or jazz piece peering out of the rubble. It was strange to see Beethoven and Mozart sandwiched between Dylan and Social Distortion. Abby wandered aimlessly through the kitchen and living room, clutching a juice glass full of Irish Mist like a Titanic survivor clinging to a lifeboat. Her eyes were red and her face streaked with tears. She switched off the high-end stereo and fixed me with a sad smile.

'I've been expecting you for the last two days,' she slurred. 'What kept you?'

I glared at her. I had walked in wanting to punch her, but something in her expression stopped me. It was the kindly, wistful look you get from your grandmother before she puts your crayon drawings on the fridge. The eyes she turned on me were deep and filled with a wisdom far beyond her age. They looked into my soul, weighed what they found and beamed at me in a non-judgmental, almost patronizing benediction.

It's hard to slam a fist into an expression like that.

'What the hell did you do to John?' I lurched on to my rant, not to be deterred.

She looked away for a moment. A new tear ran down her cheek. She raised her glass and took a long pull. 'What he needed me to,' she whispered.

That wasn't what I expected. 'He needed you to fuck his A&R guy?' I demanded.

She took another big drink, still staring at the wall that housed her record collection. It was the most vinyl I'd seen in one place since ManRay closed. When she spoke, her voice was so soft I almost missed it. 'Yes. He did.'

I snorted in what I hoped was a derisive manner.

Her meandering path took her into the spartan kitchen. She found a bottle and topped off her glass before tacking toward the living room, listing markedly to starboard. I wonder how much she'd had. I'd seen her put away beer and the occasional shot, but I'd never seen anybody swill liqueur by the cupful like this.

'Look,' she began, gesturing vaguely with the glass, 'I'm not really supposed to tell you this, and you won't believe me at first, but I think you deserve to know. And I'm really, really drunk. So I'm gonna break some rules. 'I'm John's Muse.'

'Maybe you were until…'

'I am. And for the next few weeks I shall continue to be.' She turned her tear streaked face to me. 'I hated hurting him. But he needed me to.'

'I don't know what kind of psycho-kick you're on, but that makes no sense. Maybe the booze has you rattled. Did Tom pressure you with John's career?'

She shook her head.

'Look,' she began. 'I'mma explain it slowly. One piece at a time.' She drew herself up to her full five foot one, summoning her dignity, holding her vat of amber liquor like a scepter. She looked for all the world like an Imperial Princess on a bender.

'I am far older than you could know. I am one of nine sisters, and my given name is Euterpe.'

'What the hell is that? Lebanese?'

'Greek. Our father was Zeus. For eons, it has been our task to inspire artists.'

Well, I wasn't convinced, but she sure seemed to believe what she was saying.

She smiled through her tears, 'I knew you wouldn't believe it. I mean, who would. Look, we see potential. And when we do, we nurture that. We fan the flames of raw talent until it becomes Art.'

She put such reverence into the word that I actually heard the capital letter. 'So you're saying you made John what he is?'

'Think. Before he met me he was talented. He had potential. God, did he have potential. But it was dormant. I coaxed it out of him. Without my guidance, he'd be pumping gas, playing in his garage, maybe, if he was really lucky. More likely, he'd have pawned his guitar and a dead-end job would be grinding his soul to a dull nub.'

I started to make a cutting retort, but I realized that she might have a point. It was only after he met her that he applied himself. I'd tried to get him to for years, but, the way he'd been going, the future she outlined wasn't out of the question.

'So you use your sexual wiles on poor artists and writers so they'll make something of themselves?'

'Writers?' She snorted. 'Please. Bunch of drunken egomaniacs who lack the discipline for piano lessons. I only work with musicians.'

'So you're discriminating in your slutting around?' I was getting angry now. This fairy tale stuff was pushing my buttons. The grains of truth in what she said were like salt in the wound.

She looked at me without a trace of anger. Somehow that made it worse.

'Artists need inspiration. One of the strongest inspirations, especially for musicians, is sex. So, yes, I do "slut around" with musicians, if that is what they need to drive them to create masterpieces. Sex is part of it, almost always, but most need more. John needed to be thrown into life at the deep end. He was too complacent. He only became great when he learned to live. You can't put emotion into a song when you haven't tasted it, savored it, let it run down your chin and licked the last drops from your fingers. Then, you can set it to music.'

'Look, I admit that he matured as a musician after he met you, but you're delusional,' I replied. 'You're a twenty-something groupie from Allston. You're fun and pretty, but you aren't Helen of Troy.'

'I am every woman. I am what every artist needs,' she said in perfect seriousness.

What she needed right then was an ambulance and a trip to the Bournewood Mental Hospital. Sensing my skepticism, she ran a hand though her hair and shook her head.

My jaw dropped. Her dark hair and olive skin were gone, and in their place was a fair face framed by the most amazing blonde mane I'd ever seen. Not bottle blonde, but rich shades varying from almost white to honey to shining gold. The dark eyes were deep blue now, but held the same wisdom. She was at least three inches taller and her shirt now stretched tight over a bust increased two cup sizes.

'Does this help you believe?' Her voice was deeper, richer, and carried a trace of accent I couldn't identify.

I nodded, she sighed and returned to her previous form.

'I have been many women through time. I spent the 18th century in Vienna, and the fifties in Detroit, I began the sixties in London, and ended them in San Francisco. I know every club in New York, Los Angeles, Seattle, and yes, Greater Boston. I am Euterpe. My domain is music.'

I digested this. Clearly, something out of my experience was happening. I was still angry, still confused and still didn't want to believe it.

'Why?' It was all I could come up with. 'Why leave him now? Is the thrill ride over?' I packed as much bitterness into my question as I could.

'Do you think I like to hurt people?' she asked. 'It's what he needed. It was the push. Since he signed, he's lost his edge.'

'The band is better than ever,' I retorted angrily.

'No,' she replied calmly. 'They're more polished. That's not better. The last album had about as much emotional punch as Phil Collins.' She took a deep breath and continued, 'And Tom was pushing him to blander, more commercial work. Garbage. Cheap, trite, bland garbage. Now, I've saved him from that. He'll never work with that jackal again, he'll demand more control, and the pain will come out in better music. True music. From the soul.'

'You'd hurt him for music?' I demanded.

She speared me with a gaze of pure steel. 'I've watched great artists destroy themselves, and I've helped them do it, because they needed it for their art. My job is inspiration. Some people needed sex, some drink or drugs or danger. Some couldn't produce when they were happy. They needed heartbreak to fuel their genius. Pain passes. Great works remain. The world is a better place for the suffering of a gifted few.'

I wanted to argue, to dispute such a ridiculous claim, but the look in her eyes stopped me. Was she right? Would the world be a better place if Mozart had lived a long, happy life producing mediocre music that no one could recall? If Jimi Hendrix or Charley Parker were still alive, pruning the shrubs in some suburb remembering their unremarkable dabbling in music? If Cobain had been happy and well adjusted, would Grunge have ever taken off or would bad hairmetal still be dominating the airwaves?

I couldn't help but lash out against the pain she caused, despite the obvious benefit. 'So you manipulate men to build this art? Does that get you off?'

'It's not just men, sweetie,' she smirked. 'How do you think Melissa Etheridge writes such amazing songs about unrequited love? Don't look so surprised.' She paused for a swig of booze and I suspect, dramatic effect. 'Interesting point. Regardless of sex, skill with a guitar directly correlates to skill at cunnilingus.'

'How can you do this? What do you get from it?'

'Oh, it's not for the sex or the presents or the status of being on the arm of some star. It's knowing that a song was written for you. There's no thrill to compare to that. *Come To My Window* does things to me that no lover's touch ever could. I can't hear *Born to Run* or *Thunder Road* without my legs starting to shake. I've been immortalized in song as Wendy, Mary, Peggy Sue, and Layla.'

'Not Rosanna?' I asked.

For the first time, through all the insults I had flung her way, I saw her angry.

'Toto?' She spat the word through clenched teeth. If looks could kill, I'd have dropped on the spot. 'What the hell do you think I am?'

Well, we both knew the answer to that, but apparently she had standards.

Her anger was short-lived. She walked unsteadily back to the kitchen, retrieved another glass and sloshed an unreasonable amount of spirit into it before extending it toward me. 'Here. You're gonna need this.'

I accepted the glass hesitantly and took a sip.

She leaned against the kitchen counter to stop the sway she had acquired somewhere over the last six ounces. 'I have to apologize to you. I know I hurt him, and I hurt you. If I'd stayed away, you two would be together. Wait, let me finish. I couldn't let that happen. Not at that moment. I told you we Muses can see potential. I saw his, and I saw yours. We also see need. For where he was, for as mature as he was, or wasn't as the case may be, you couldn't give him what he needed. You weren't wild enough and you weren't cruel enough,' she almost sobbed, but caught herself. 'It's not about giving him what he wants, it's about giving him what he needs. I did what I had to do to get him to where he is, and now to get him out of this rut. I had to burn bridges to do it. I can't ever go back. He's your project now. But here's what I left you.' She walked to the stereo.

'What do you mean?'

'This is the rough cut of what he's been working on. I got a copy. I know people.'

She pushed a button on the stereo.

The song that played was maybe a bit rough. Just a bit, but the lyrics were poetry, and the pain just poured out of the speakers.

I was speechless. That was the best he'd ever sounded. Better than I ever imagined he could.

She fixed me with that ageless gaze though red-rimmed eyes, her face a mask of pride and sorrow.

When the song finished, she said, 'That. That is what he's capable of. Make sure he remembers that.'

I could only nod dumbly.

She stood, wobbling a bit.

'I'm going to bed. You can let yourself out. Do your best with him.'

I nodded again.

'There are rewards you know,' she smirked. 'He's a very good guitarist.'

* * * *

Six months later, John and I were sharing a table at the Middle East, taking in a new act. She was a folk rock, acoustic solo act. Very soulful, competent musician. I had the feeling that she could go places.

As we listened, I noticed a curvy little blonde with a short, spiked haircut dancing in front of the stage in a tight Indigo Girls t shirt and low rider jeans, a tribal tattoo displayed on a swath of bare back. Her eyes were fixed on the singer as she swayed in time to the music, her sinuous movements speaking volumes of lascivious promise.

While I'd never met the girl, there was something oddly familiar about her.

'You know,' I told John, 'I think this girl's going places.'

'Really?' he asked. 'I suppose she has some potential.'

'All she needs is the right inspiration.'

'You think she'll find it?'

'Somehow I do,' I replied. 'And, you know, she plays a pretty good guitar.'

Iwokrama

Girdharry

You know that trick you can do with your mind, when you convince yourself you're not afraid of heights? I do it myself so I know it works. Or rather, it works until you look down.

Flimsy boards, suspended by knotted rope, form a pathway through the air. So uninviting, the bridge stretches before my feet, from one huge tree to another one a long way away.

'It's easy, don't be frightened.'

Yeah, right. Should I really believe my twenty-something, Amerindian guide? I think he means easy for him.

The rainforest canopy walkway, Iwokrama. I'm surrounded by eighty percent humidity. Is that even possible? Sweat takes advantage and drenches my body. From the tree ahead, our guide smiles back his encouragement. I stare at him, caught in the spell of his lightness, his ease. Between us, the bridge sways and creaks.

Did I mention the anti-malarials yet? Polluting my bloodstream, they create a deadly environment for parasites. A deadly environment for my kidneys too, I suspect.

'This is the best one,' the practice nurse had promised me. 'Absolutely the least side effects.'

Sure, that is if you don't count dizziness, nausea and a newly-discovered balance problem. In a moment of disorientation, I'd almost impaled myself on a metal post back in Georgetown.

Sweat slicks my back. Green, leaf-filtered light plays with my mind. Myriad, exotic bird calls fall on me like hot rain. I'm in a bath of melody and sheer volume. I don't care anymore, not about the dizziness, not about the bridge. A flash of blue and orange. Two macaws alight close by. The spirit of the rainforest dances.

I step out.

TALES OF THE SHONRI: PRIDE AIN'T NOTHING

STEPHEN GODDEN

I SEEN THE MANTA COMING over the river. Big creature, skin black as coal dust, flapping some, losing some, carrying the rich folks down across the water. Long, slow, brown water, rolling, rolling, carrying the deadness down. Manta flopped a bit. Flapped a bit. Fell a bit. Magic caught it again after the brown water passed on by beneath its guts. Lifted it up, the magic strong now, then the Manta swooped. Our job now. Us slaves. Gotsta tie it down and not get ate.

'Dance quick,' I said to Kera. 'Keep away from that mouth.'

She nodded. Good girl, Kera, not her fault she got branded. Crossed the wrong mage. Didn't like his smelly breath on her. Ends up here — like me. Only I punched a mage's little helper that liked little boys. Not hard, but hard enough to get 'im off me. Long time back now. Been slaving a long long time, but never whoring. They can kill me afore I do that. I'll take a few with me, too. They knows that, leaves me be, wild eyes I got, see.

Here it comes.

Manta swooping.

Gotsta be careful now.

Gotsta.

We sprinted out as it dropped closer. Closer. Ropes in our hands. Dancing under the bottom of the Manta. Ships they calls them, Manta-ships. Just Manta to us. Poor beasty, bloated up, pumped full of magic, born from the sea but riding the waves of magic in the sky. Ain't seen the sea in a long time, poor beasty, makes it nasty, sharp teeth, all shark, eat you up if you dance slow.

I got the rope, thick as my arm, over my shoulder. Kera got the hook. Been a dance team a while now, but I seen that look in her eye. That look that says, 'Enough.'

She looked at me now, her eyes close by, tears. 'Goodbye, Gwil,' she said, then she dropped the hook, lost the dance, threw herself at the Manta's mouth.

Chomp.

And she'd gone.

I grabbed the hook. Kept dancing. Hard on your own. Needs two really. Rope's heavy. Hook's sharp. I'm strong though. Spin the hook. Throw it high. Let it catch in the skin of the Manta. It don't make no sound, fish don't, don't need to cry out in the sea.

The hook dug in. Bit of blood, not much, good enough. I danced away from the mouth, let go of the rope. It tightened as the big men started to pull.

Other dance pairs, small, light, quick as me, threw their hooks, caught the Manta, tied it down. I ran back to the slave post and took a drink of water to clear the dust from my throat. Threw some over my face to clear the tears from my eyes.

'Bit of protein for the ship, hey,' the overseer said, laughing. I looked at him. He backed away. 'She weren't nothing but a slave,' he sneered, but he kept right on backing.

Rich folk clambered down the steps, stuck hard into the side of the Manta, stitched into its hide, wounding it. Ain't the beasty's fault, no sir. Kera died coz of them, the rich folks, the bosses, the Mages. They got other twisted-up little beasties with them. Some to guard, some to carry, some to whore.

Broke the world they did, the Mages. Only the Shonri fight back against them. Other people just duck their heads, knuckle their foreheads, don't look, don't see, don't ask, don't tell, don't do nothing as the world goes to hell.

I ran away that night. Overseer dead behind me, strangled with his own guts. 'Bit of protein,' I whispered as his lips went blue.

* * * *

Steam puffs out of the smoke stack; big old wheels on the corners of the boat, turning, wet, slick, sound like a waterfall. They calls her the Mary.

Paddle-ship. Goes where the magic can't, up past the Drowned City.

Captain took me on easy like. Didn't care about the brand. Cook took care of that. Big hot knife from the galley. Sizzle, smell like bacon cooking. I passed out, but I weren't no slave no more when I woke. Captain takes on any to work the ships. Any that's good with ropes. I'm good with ropes. I can dance with them.

So the Mary ran up and down the river. Long, slow, brown water, carrying the deadness away from the City. That there was a sight.

The City.

Towers, fallen, old rusted steel and iron, like the bones of a dead man still scraping at the sky. Deep channels between the towers, but gotsta be careful of snags. Steel bones always falling off the towers. Breaking away. Captain says the Mages did this. Built this place. Then the magic failed in their war. Too much taken. Just fell away. And the river rose. Broke its banks. Washed away all the stuff, all the streets. Captain says there's money down there. Gold, copper, jewels, but there's other things too. Things the magic changed as it died. Don't fall in there, the captain says. You'll never come back out.

I ain't Kera. I ain't gonna say 'enough'. I wants me some pay-back.

It's hard to hide what lies behind my eyes sometimes when the Mages, and the bosses, and their doxy girls'n'boys come aboard. They use the Mary to get to the place where the magic rises again. From a Manta to the Mary then back to a Manta once we're upstream of the deadness. Captain never takes them through the City though. Not the Magekin and their type. Only goes to the City when she's aboard.

She stood at the bow of the boat. All day. All night. Cloaked. Unmoving. Staring at the river as it rolled on by. Don't know her name or who she is, but the Captain, he leaves her be, so that's good enough for me.

Then.

One time.

She and a Mage were aboard together.

Trouble tanged the air like rain-smell.

The Mage was the fighting type, all brown armour and dead eyes. Not eyes like mine, not wild eyes, not eyes that'd keep on glaring as the light died behind them. She had eyes like mine. Mine were brown and hers were blue, sharp-blue like old ice, but they were like mine all right. Saw them when she came aboard once. Boat shifted. I thought she'd fall off the gangway, slung a rope for her to catch. Slung it fast like, but she didn't need it. Barely even seemed to notice the wobble of the plank.

Blade, long, thin, sparkling, hissed out from under that cloak. Cut the rope in twain. So fast. Barely saw the blade, barely saw her move, but saw her eyes. She looked at me for a long second. I didn't back up, but I wanted to. Eyes like mine only deeper, darker, brighter, and lined with silver threads.

Shonri!

I didn't back up and she smiled. The blade gone. Back under her cloak. Like it never existed at all.

The Mage had lizard-men bodyguards with him. Kirruk, the Captain called 'em. Nasty things. Not nasty like the Manta were nasty, coz of pain and such; no, nasty coz they liked it.

One time, one of them were being nasty to the Cook's girl. No lust in it, not for sex anyway. He'd have hurt her bad, but he slipped on a rope, slung fast like under his feet, then whipped away. He fell overboard into the water, screamed like a crow biting at eagles as he got dragged down.

His Mage got angry. Blistering, like a snake, high on his ego, on his rights, but Cook said, and Captain said, he must've just fallen. Maybe he thought he was cleverer than he was, maybe that made him fall. Nothing to be done.

The Cook always fed me well after that.

So the air tanged with violence and she stood at the bow of the boat. Cloaked. Unmoving. Staring at the river as it rolled on by.

The Mage and his Kirruks came out on the deck behind her. Steam puffs out of the smoke stack; big old wheel on the back of the boat, turning, wet, slick, sound like a waterfall.

And she stood, cloaked, unmoving, as they circled around her.

I picked me up a rope.

Always good with ropes, me. I can dance with them.

Captain shook his head. Wanted me to not look, not see, not move, not act.

I wanted me some payback.

Cook burned away my brand. I weren't no slave no more. 'Enough,' she said, and lost the hook, lost the dance, threw herself at the poor beasty's mouth.

Chomp.

The Mage pulled out something. All brass and hissy. Aimed it at her.

And she moved. Cloak fell away. Two blades: long, thin, sparkling, hissing through the air.

The brass, hissy thing fell, cut in twain, onto the deck, where it began to smoke. The Mage threw himself back. Away from her. Away from her eyes, those wild eyes, just like mine, only sharp, blue, like old ice. Lined with silver. Silver that glowed, that flowed around every sinew, every muscle, every nerve in her body.

Shonri.

Awakened.

Deadly.

Killing fast.

Not much time for my payback. Not when those blades were hissing out the tang-beat of violence. I slung me rope. Hooked it around the Mage's neck. Pulled it tight. A loop, such a loop. He's heavy, old, fat; I'm strong though. Spin the rope. Spin him out from behind his dying lizards. Brace hard. Twist. Flop. Flip. Throw.

Over he goes.

Into the water.

I look.

I see it. Rising below him.

Anac snake. Long, strong, big as a Manta. Sharp teeth.

Free.

Chomp.

* * * *

'My name is Terin,' she said. 'Why did you do that?'

'Wanted me some payback.' I showed her where Cook had burned the brand away.

'A slave with pride,' she said, a razored edge within the laugh.

'Pride ain't nothing.'

'That's a double negative,' she said.

'What's a double… whatever?'
'If pride ain't nothing then it must be something.'
'Ain't wrong then, am I?'

More *Tales of the Shonri* are available at **www.writerlot.net** and the novella *Tales of the Shonri: City of Lights* is available from Firedance Books.

THE SIGN

JANET ALLISON BROWN

S O, OKAY, I WAS SITTING IN THIS BAR. Now you're going to think that's the main point of this story — me, in a bar, right? But that's not the story, Sam. Pay attention.

I was in this bar, minding my own business, sort of, and this woman came and sat down next to me. She was pretty, about my age, with smudged mascara. And I thought: there's a woman beside me, and she's been crying, and we're in a bar, so obviously she wants to talk. So I handed her a napkin, in a gesture of sisterhood, and she said thank you, and we got talking.

And she told me she'd just left her husband. I asked her, why did you leave him? My whole marriage was based on a lie, she said. I asked her, what was the lie? And she told me.

They had been courting for about two years, which is about the same time as you and me, Sam, right? So they'd been courting and she wasn't sure about him. I mean, she loved him, sort of, but she wasn't sure about marrying him. So one day she came home from work at lunchtime — her home, Sam; they didn't live together before they were married, not like you and me. So she came home early, to her house — because she had a headache, jeez, I don't know — and guess what? There on her doorstep was a small bunch of flowers, and a note that said, I love you Caroline — that was her name, Caroline — I love you Caroline and I want you to be my wife.

So, really sweet, right? That's what she thought: really sweet. And more than that, it was a sign. She never came home at lunchtime, never, and this one time she had, and it was exactly the same day that he had chosen to leave the flowers there for her. If she hadn't come home then, she'd have missed them, because the school kids come right by her house at the end of the day, and they'd have taken the flowers for sure. And she was thinking, thank God I came home today, it was meant to be, thank you, God, that was the sign I was waiting for. And she married him.

So they're married for ten years. Ten years, Sam, that's eight years, three months and sixteen days longer than you and me. Ten years they're married, and one day she says to him, thank God for the sign that sent me home that day, or I'd have missed your flowers and proposal and we'd never have had this happy marriage.

And he starts to laugh and she says, what? And he says, you don't think I left it to chance, do you? I left you flowers every day for nearly six months, so that if you ever came home at lunchtime you'd find them and you'd know how much I love you.

She said to me, well, I thought about it and thought about it, and after a time I realised my whole marriage was based on a lie.

Do you see, Sam? She thought it was a sign, and it was no such thing, he'd been leaving her flowers every day. That's not a sign, that's dogged persistence. So she left him, and she's going to get a divorce, and that's the end of her marriage.

So that was me in a bar. But wait, pay attention, there's more. A few days later I was in a bar again. I know, I know — me, in a bar! But I had such an interesting time the first time, I figured I might get lucky twice. So I sat there with my drink, waiting, waiting, and this nice-looking guy sits down next to me. So I said, do you want to talk? Oh yeah, he says. You're a woman. I need to talk to a woman about my wife. I told him, I'm all ears.

So he'd been in love with the same girl all his life, right? The same girl. Not like you, Sam, who went out with just about every pretty girl in town and some of the ugly ones too. So he's in love with her and she's all popular and he doesn't dare to ask her out, and then one day, out of the blue, she sits down beside him at the cinema and they get talking and soon they're seeing each other regularly. And he's really in love, you know, but he doesn't know if she feels the same way. He thinks she does, but he isn't sure.

Are you keeping up, Sam? Pay attention. So he comes up with a plan. He's going to do something to win her heart. He thinks and he thinks and this is what he comes up with. Every morning he gets up early and he goes walking in the fields, and he picks a little posy of flowers. Nothing fancy, just a modest posy, gathered with love. Then he parks a street away from her house, and watches until she leaves for work. The minute she's gone, he puts the flowers on her porch, with a note asking her to marry him.

He knows that the flowers will wilt by the end of the day. He knows the school kids pass by her house every afternoon, and they'll probably take the flowers anyway. He knows she never comes home for lunch. But he's working hard to buy a nice house for her, and early mornings are the only spare time he has, so he has to take a chance. He figures he'll just keep on leaving the flowers and the notes and eventually she'll find them and then she'll understand how much he loves her.

Six months. This carries on for six months. That's a lot of getting up early and waiting for her to leave her house. That's a lot of flowers. That's dedication. And finally it paid off.

He tells me, we had ten beautiful years. They were the happiest years of my life. And now she's left me. She left me because I left the flowers every day. I don't understand. I couldn't have tried any harder.

So Sam, those are the stories I heard in the bar. Did you notice? They were the same story. It was the same story, told from both sides. See, he won her hand in marriage because he tried so hard. And he lost it because he tried so hard. She married her guy because of a sign, and it was a sign, but it wasn't from God, it was from her husband, who'd loved her all his life.

So here's the thing, Sam. I've been thinking and thinking about this — the same story, two sides. And I've decided, maybe, that's what's wrong between you and me. See, you and that naked girl in our bed — maybe that's just my side of the story. Maybe you've got another side, one that will make this hole in my heart just seal right over like it was never there. You'll tell me your side of why that girl had no clothes on and why you and she were in our bed, and I'll say, oh, that's what happened? Sam, my love, what a fool I've been!

Because I'm not like that woman in the bar, Sam. I need no signs. With me it's effort that counts; I'll take effort every time. So sock it to me. I'm all ears. Tell me your side of the story, so I never have to set foot in another bar. 'Cause you know, me, in a bar, right?

THE SUMMONING

ISSY FLAMEL

COLD SNAKES OF FOG WRITHE from the sluggish flow of the Thames, deadening the clip-clop of the carriage horses that trot past in the gloom, harnesses clinking as they dissolve into the mists of Soho.

'Shilling for one of the Six Hundred, Sir? First to the guns for Queen and country.' The beggar thrusts a battered army cap forward with a reek of sour ale, his grimy eye-patch, set in a sea of scars that disfigure a shattered cheek and jaw, breaking into the flickering glare of the gaslights. Tennyson only published in The Examiner days ago, and surely this wretch cannot have been shipped from the Crimea in six weeks? But he gets a sixpence for sheer gall, and raises a knuckle to his temple as he turns for the gin-shop at the corner of Wardour Street.

A siren voice calls from the warm light under a painted sign announcing Mrs Dawson's Dress Emporium.

'Care for a fitting, dearie? You look a well-built fellow.' she trills, swishing her skirts so the material gleams in invitation. An acceptance will win passage through the veil of heavy velvet curtains at the rear of the shop, revealing the narrow stairwell up which the real business is conducted. Under her feet, entombed in the dripping walls of the basement room, two sullen-eyed waifs watch as their mother vomits her life away while *Vibrio cholarae* breeds inside her. The industrious Pacini has this same year identified the germ through his microscopical investigations, but what can a subject of the medieval fantasia that is Lombardy-Venetia know of medicine? Doctor Snow, who cannot be doubted on the grounds of being a feverish Latin, has also produced his outlandish theory of little unseen creatures; but everyone knows the science is settled and a miasma of foul breezes transmits the disease.

So although the handle was removed from the pump on Broad Street in September, other sources of infection remain. They will all be buried in the same grave, as the parish coffers of St. Luke's are drained by the epidemic.

Next door to the bawdy den the grey stones and leaded windows are covered in a spreading crust of green algae, as though nature is rebelling against the artifice of human ingenuity and reclaiming the façade. The curious potential customer extracts his handkerchief and wipes clear a viewing hole into the dank interior. He makes out an eccentric jumble of bric-a-brac, furniture and dusty piles of leather-bound manuscripts. A balding toy monkey sits expectantly, cymbals poised to clash, waiting for the maestro's acknowledgement. Beside it, a pair of russet enamel vases, one with an umbrella poking out of the top, the other blessed with a cascade of curling, desiccated lilac blooms, the promise of their heady, sultry perfume enticing one over the threshold through the glass. And perched atop a French Empire escritoire, oval eyes glinting in the reflected brilliance of gold-leaf patterning, squats a lacquerware demon. His tongue protrudes rudely between razor teeth, lolling down onto his blood-red chest as his gaze beckons. Entering, as under a spell, the traveller falls into the darkness of another world.

ABOUT THE CONTRIBUTORS

A salesman for most of his adult life, ALF HAYWOOD has decided to brush off retirement in favour of being a full-time writer. He started writing romance and adventure stories about three years ago. Now his mission is to prove to his wife and family that all those hours huddled over a computer in his office were not wasted.

ALISON GARDINER writes YA novels, picture books, non-fiction, women's fiction, film scripts: a polygenre. Four children keep her in touch with her readers and technology, out of touch with her bank balance and any chance of a calm, sensible life. For which she is grateful. Loving travelling, fantasy, mystery, laughter means there is a constant swirl of stories inside her head and it's a brilliant feeling to let them flow out. Broadcasting weekly on Radio Litopia gives her the chance to chat to many authors, which keeps her dreaming. Life is too short to be serious.

WILLIAM WEBB JNR is an SFF — short, fat and fifty. He believes life's passion lies within absurdity, that Douglas Adams was a prophet, Pratchett is a genius, and Irma Bombeck died too soon. Along with a lifetime of experience as a CFO (not bad for someone with a marketing degree), he is also a writer for regional papers. His fiction is a rambunctious mix of sci-fi and humour.

BILL "BOOPADOO" SAUER is a former musician, former photographer, graphic designer by day, and writer by night and weekend. He has scribbled down millions of words since childhood. The words just come, and who are we to try and stop them? Husband, brother to a legion of siblings, doggie daddy to mutts and strays. Often mistaken for a big, dumb gorilla until proven otherwise, which is how Bill likes it. Then it's always a pleasant surprise when the truth is discovered: that boy can write, can't he? Especially when it's Bill doing the discovering.

Born and raised all over the southern United States — yet somehow surviving with her higher senses generally intact — CAT COFFEY now resides in the sticky, throbbing heart of American dreams and nightmares, New York City. After a stint as a starving non-artist working in stage theatre management, she now enjoys the plush life of a sellout working in real estate. She writes to keep herself sane. Amateur psychiatric tests indicate that she should probably write more.

COLIN F. BARNES is a writer (and publisher with Anachron Press) of horror, crime and speculative fiction. He takes his influence from everyday life, and the weird happenings that go on in the shadowy locales of Essex in the UK.
Website: www.colinfbarnes.com
Publisher: www.anachronpress.com

GARY BONN lives in Scotland with his family and an alarming number of accident-prone chickens. His writing is informed by his long experience working with children with social, behavioural or mental health difficulties and equally by his fascination with hunter-gatherer societies. He throws a mean spear. Gary's first novel *Expect Civilian Casualties* is published by Firedance Books.

GIRDHARRY is in her fourth decade and lives an ordinary life with two children and one husband. She spent a great deal of her early years, restless, unhappy, searching for something-but-she-didn't-know-what, and on her journeys, popping into the occasional therapy clinic or tai chi class. She discovered some fascinating aspects of life and it's these ideas which inspire her writing.

ISLAND WRITER produces non-fiction for WriterLot about the reality of living in the West Indies, rather than the sugar-coated view of the tourist. She is British, married to an American. She and her husband moved to the tiny island of Antigua, in the West Indies, from London in 2004, to experience a better quality of life. After all, we come this way only once.

ISSY FLAMEL is an infant dipsomaniac, who has high hopes of being a polymath when he grows up.

JANET ALLISON BROWN is the author of dozens of children's picture books and editor of several volumes of academic papers. She has written explorer guides, restaurant reviews, and articles on a range of subjects including traditional Arabic ship-building and handicrafts, adoption, education, faith and ancient cave paintings. Wife, mother, home-educator, writer and editor, she was educated at Balliol College, Oxford, and lives in rural Derbyshire. She likes stories, and makes them up all the time. Her novel, *The Walker's Daughter,* is published by Firedance Books.

LOUISE COLE is older than she behaves but younger than she looks. Over-educated and totally lacking in financial ambition, she has nevertheless managed to hold down various jobs in journalism and publishing. She finally forsook the lure of a regular paycheck to run her own media agency in North Yorkshire, thinking that quality time with her family and her writing would more than compensate for the lack of money. Yeah, well, you have to try these things. Louise contributes shorts to WriterLot. Her first novel, the YA paranormal thriller *The Devil's Poetry* will be out soon.

PATRICK LECLERC makes good use of his history degree by working as a paramedic for an ever-changing parade of ambulance companies in the Northern suburbs of Boston. When not writing he enjoys cooking, fencing and making witty, insightful remarks with career-limiting candor. Patrick LeClerc's first novel, *Out of Nowhere,* is published by Firedance Books.

REN WAROM is a writer of speculative oddities, not known for an ability to fit into boxes of any description. She's a certified Pirate-nun, mum to three spawn, slave to several cats, writing obsessive and general weirdo. The word *askance* was invented for the way people tend to look at her. For her sins, Ren is now represented by the fabulous Jennifer Udden of the Donald Maass Literary Agency. At some point, evidence of this union will land in a bookshop near you. It's recommended you buy hazard gear in preparation.

STEVE GODDEN writes speculative fiction. He reads pretty much anything. He uses the second to fuel the first. (And writes this stuff in the third, because somebody told him once that he should and he didn't like to argue.) Other than that, Steve's just a bloke of independent penury and incidental personality. He also writes under the name T F Grant. Well, gotta have some variety in your life. Steve's novella, *Tales of the Shonri: City of Lights,* is published by Firedance Books.

ALSO AVAILABLE!

Available from Firedance Books...

THE WALKER'S DAUGHTER by Janet Allison Brown.

When her mother dies at the hands of a silver-haired figure in black, six-year-old spirit-walker Cora Bloux hides out in her own body. Twenty years later she's still there, fiercely maintaining an outwardly stable, conventional life.

But when her own daughter is hit by a car, Cora is forced to spirit-walk again — and discovers that the spirit world has been waiting for her.

In the extraordinary, fast-paced world of spirit-walkers, body-swappers, rock bands and second chances, Cora must discover her true self and learn the ordinary lessons of courage, trust and love.

To see the world as it really is, sometimes you have to close your eyes and... walk.

"This supernatural begins with a bang."
Publisher's Weekly

"Intense and enlightening."
ABNA (Amazon Breakthrough Novel Award) 2011 Expert Reviewer

Also Available!

Available from Firedance Books...

OUT OF NOWHERE by Patrick LeClerc.

An urban fantasy, pacy, funny and compelling to the last page...

Healer Sean Danet is immortal — a fact he has cloaked for centuries, behind army lines and now a paramedic's uniform. Having forgotten most of his distant past, he has finally found peace — and love.

But there are some things you cannot escape, however much distance you put behind you. When Sean heals the wrong man, he uncovers a lethal enemy who holds all the cards. And this time he can't run.

It's time to stand and fight, for himself, for his friends, for the woman he loves. It's time, finally, for Sean to face his past — and choose a future.

A story of love, of battle — and of facing your true self when there's nowhere left to hide.

"Captivating. Fans of Jim Butcher, Kim Harrison or great urban fantasy will love this."
Louise Cole, WRM

"A sharp thriller with profound insights and subtle wit. Another one for my favourites bookshelf."
Gary Bonn, author of *Expect Civilian Casualties*

Also Available!

Available from Firedance Books...

EXPECT CIVILIAN CASUALTIES by Gary Bonn.

Jason has spent the last six years living wild on beaches. Now he's seventeen and a feral girl walks into his life.

A girl with no name.

He calls her Anna. She's fun, she's kind — and she's the most dangerous person in the world.

The most unusual love story, and a truly strange war story... Expect Civilian Casualties turns how we see the world upside down.

"Bonn's writing is like biting into a lime — fresh, zesty and bitter-sweet. Seeing the world through Jason's eyes is a revelation."
Louise Cole, WRM

"A story about a boy on the edge of society who finds love and belonging in the midst of chaos and horror. A delight."
Julie Erwin: *of Altered States* contributor

Also Available!

Available from Firedance Books...

TALES OF THE SHONRI: CITY OF LIGHTS by Stephen Godden.

Darkness never falls in the City of Lights. The last hope of a broken world, the remaining Shonri warriors brave the ever-vigilant city to fight their war against the vicious Magi — or meet their deaths. For the last witch Medina, powerful, seductive, and untrustworthy, has sold her art to their enemies.

Can the handful of Shonri end the battle before Medina's magic reveals them? Can Medina survive her attempts to use the Magi for her own means? And can any of them live with the results of the battle they are about to face...

For while they scheme and fight, something stirs beneath the City of Lights... something more perilous than death itself...

Also Available!

Available from Firedance Books...

BROKEN WORLDS Volume One.

What happens when you challenge fifteen writers from around the globe to share their interpretation of a 'broken world'? They take us on a strange and wondrous journey through techno-futures, divine and diabolical games, heartbreak, murder, madness and regret. But they also show us the depths of insight, compassion, love and faith, which shine brightest in the darkest of places.

These stories span all genres: cyberpunk, literary fiction, thriller, romance, spec-fic, sci-fi and absurdist comedy.